GStreamer Plugin Writer's Guide (1.10.1)

Richard John Boulton

Erik Walthinsen

Steve Baker

Leif Johnson

Ronald S. Bultje

Stefan Kost

Tim-Philipp Müller

Wim Taymans

GStreamer Plugin Writer's Guide (1.10.1)

by Richard John Boulton, Erik Walthinsen, Steve Baker, Leif Johnson, Ronald S. Bultje, Stefan Kost, Tim-Philipp Müller, and Wim Taymans

Table of Contents

List of Tables

I. Introduction

GStreamer is an extremely powerful and versatile framework for creating streaming media applications. Many of the virtues of the GStreamer framework come from its modularity: GStreamer can seamlessly incorporate new plugin modules. But because modularity and power often come at a cost of greater complexity (consider, for example, CORBA (http://www.omg.org/)), writing new plugins is not always easy.

This guide is intended to help you understand the GStreamer framework (version 1.10.1) so you can develop new plugins to extend the existing functionality. The guide addresses most issues by following the development of an example plugin - an audio filter plugin - written in C. However, the later parts of the guide also present some issues involved in writing other types of plugins, and the end of the guide describes some of the Python bindings for GStreamer.

Chapter 1. Preface

1.1. What is GStreamer?

GStreamer is a framework for creating streaming media applications. The fundamental design comes from the video pipeline at Oregon Graduate Institute, as well as some ideas from DirectShow.

GStreamer's development framework makes it possible to write any type of streaming multimedia application. The GStreamer framework is designed to make it easy to write applications that handle audio or video or both. It isn't restricted to audio and video, and can process any kind of data flow. The pipeline design is made to have little overhead above what the applied filters induce. This makes GStreamer a good framework for designing even high-end audio applications which put high demands on latency or performance.

One of the most obvious uses of GStreamer is using it to build a media player. GStreamer already includes components for building a media player that can support a very wide variety of formats, including MP3, Ogg/Vorbis, MPEG-1/2, AVI, Quicktime, mod, and more. GStreamer, however, is much more than just another media player. Its main advantages are that the pluggable components can be mixed and matched into arbitrary pipelines so that it's possible to write a full-fledged video or audio editing application.

The framework is based on plugins that will provide the various codec and other functionality. The plugins can be linked and arranged in a pipeline. This pipeline defines the flow of the data.

The GStreamer core function is to provide a framework for plugins, data flow, synchronization and media type handling/negotiation. It also provides an API to write applications using the various plugins.

1.2. Who Should Read This Guide?

This guide explains how to write new modules for GStreamer. The guide is relevant to several groups of people:

- Anyone who wants to add support for new ways of processing data in GStreamer. For example, a person in this group might want to create a new data format converter, a new visualization tool, or a new decoder or encoder.

- Anyone who wants to add support for new input and output devices. For example, people in this group might want to add the ability to write to a new video output system or read data from a digital camera or special microphone.

- Anyone who wants to extend GStreamer in any way. You need to have an understanding of how the plugin system works before you can understand the constraints that the plugin system places on the rest of the code. Also, you might be surprised after reading this at how much can be done with plugins.

This guide is not relevant to you if you only want to use the existing functionality of GStreamer, or if you just want to use an application that uses GStreamer. If you are only interested in using existing plugins to write a new application - and there are quite a lot of plugins already - you might want to check the *GStreamer Application Development Manual*. If you are just trying to get help with a GStreamer application, then you should check with the user manual for that particular application.

1.3. Preliminary Reading

This guide assumes that you are somewhat familiar with the basic workings of GStreamer. For a gentle introduction to programming concepts in GStreamer, you may wish to read the *GStreamer Application Development Manual* first. Also check out the other documentation available on the GStreamer web site (http://gstreamer.freedesktop.org/documentation/).

In order to understand this manual, you will need to have a basic understanding of the C language. Since GStreamer adheres to the GObject programming model, this guide also assumes that you understand the basics of GObject (http://developer.gnome.org/gobject/stable/pt01.html) programming. You may also want to have a look at Eric Harlow's book *Developing Linux Applications with GTK+ and GDK*.

1.4. Structure of This Guide

To help you navigate through this guide, it is divided into several large parts. Each part addresses a particular broad topic concerning GStreamer plugin development. The parts of this guide are laid out in the following order:

- Building a Plugin - Introduction to the structure of a plugin, using an example audio filter for illustration.

  This part covers all the basic steps you generally need to perform to build a plugin, such as registering the element with GStreamer and setting up the basics so it can receive data from and send data to neighbour elements. The discussion begins by giving examples of generating the basic structures and registering an element in Constructing the Boilerplate. Then, you will learn how to write the code to get a basic filter plugin working in Chapter 4, Chapter 5 and Chapter 8.

  After that, we will show some of the GObject concepts on how to make an element configurable for applications and how to do application-element interaction in Adding Properties and Chapter 10. Next, you will learn to build a quick test application to test all that you've just learned in Chapter 11. We will just touch upon basics here. For full-blown application development, you should look at the Application Development Manual (http://gstreamer.freedesktop.org/data/doc/gstreamer/head/manual/html/index.html).

• Advanced Filter Concepts - Information on advanced features of GStreamer plugin development.

After learning about the basic steps, you should be able to create a functional audio or video filter plugin with some nice features. However, GStreamer offers more for plugin writers. This part of the guide includes chapters on more advanced topics, such as scheduling, media type definitions in GStreamer, clocks, interfaces and tagging. Since these features are purpose-specific, you can read them in any order, most of them don't require knowledge from other sections.

The first chapter, named Different scheduling modes, will explain some of the basics of element scheduling. It is not very in-depth, but is mostly some sort of an introduction on why other things work as they do. Read this chapter if you're interested in GStreamer internals. Next, we will apply this knowledge and discuss another type of data transmission than what you learned in Chapter 5: Different scheduling modes. Loop-based elements will give you more control over input rate. This is useful when writing, for example, muxers or demuxers.

Next, we will discuss media identification in GStreamer in Chapter 16. You will learn how to define new media types and get to know a list of standard media types defined in GStreamer.

In the next chapter, you will learn the concept of request- and sometimes-pads, which are pads that are created dynamically, either because the application asked for it (request) or because the media stream requires it (sometimes). This will be in Chapter 12.

The next chapter, Chapter 18, will explain the concept of clocks in GStreamer. You need this information when you want to know how elements should achieve audio/video synchronization.

The next few chapters will discuss advanced ways of doing application-element interaction. Previously, we learned on the GObject-ways of doing this in Adding Properties and Chapter 10. We will discuss dynamic parameters, which are a way of defining element behaviour over time in advance, in Chapter 20. Next, you will learn about interfaces in Chapter 21. Interfaces are very target- specific ways of application-element interaction, based on GObject's GInterface. Lastly, you will learn about how metadata is handled in GStreamer in Chapter 22.

The last chapter, Chapter 17, will discuss the concept of events in GStreamer. Events are, on the one hand, another way of doing application-element interaction. It takes care of seeking, for example. On the other hand, it is also a way in which elements interact with each other, such as letting each other know about media stream discontinuities, forwarding tags inside a pipeline and so on.

• Creating special element types - Explanation of writing other plugin types.

Because the first two parts of the guide use an audio filter as an example, the concepts introduced apply to filter plugins. But many of the concepts apply equally to other plugin types, including sources, sinks, and autopluggers. This part of the guide presents the issues that arise when working on these more specialized plugin types. The chapter starts with a special focus on elements that can be written using a base-class (Pre-made base classes), and later also goes into writing special types of elements in Writing a Demuxer or Parser, Writing a N-to-1 Element or Muxer and Writing a Manager.

- Appendices - Further information for plugin developers.

  The appendices contain some information that stubbornly refuses to fit cleanly in other sections of the guide. Most of this section is not yet finished.

The remainder of this introductory part of the guide presents a short overview of the basic concepts involved in GStreamer plugin development. Topics covered include Elements and Plugins, Pads, Data, Buffers and Events and Types and Properties. If you are already familiar with this information, you can use this short overview to refresh your memory, or you can skip to Building a Plugin.

As you can see, there a lot to learn, so let's get started!

- Creating compound and complex elements by extending from a GstBin. This will allow you to create plugins that have other plugins embedded in them.
- Adding new media types to the registry along with typedetect functions. This will allow your plugin to operate on a completely new media type.

Chapter 2. Foundations

This chapter of the guide introduces the basic concepts of GStreamer. Understanding these concepts will help you grok the issues involved in extending GStreamer. Many of these concepts are explained in greater detail in the *GStreamer Application Development Manual*; the basic concepts presented here serve mainly to refresh your memory.

2.1. Elements and Plugins

Elements are at the core of GStreamer. In the context of plugin development, an *element* is an object derived from the GstElement (../../gstreamer/html/GstElement.html) class. Elements provide some sort of functionality when linked with other elements: For example, a source element provides data to a stream, and a filter element acts on the data in a stream. Without elements, GStreamer is just a bunch of conceptual pipe fittings with nothing to link. A large number of elements ship with GStreamer, but extra elements can also be written.

Just writing a new element is not entirely enough, however: You will need to encapsulate your element in a *plugin* to enable GStreamer to use it. A plugin is essentially a loadable block of code, usually called a shared object file or a dynamically linked library. A single plugin may contain the implementation of several elements, or just a single one. For simplicity, this guide concentrates primarily on plugins containing one element.

A *filter* is an important type of element that processes a stream of data. Producers and consumers of data are called *source* and *sink* elements, respectively. *Bin* elements contain other elements. One type of bin is responsible for synchronization of the elements that they contain so that data flows smoothly. Another type of bin, called *autoplugger* elements, automatically add other elements to the bin and links them together so that they act as a filter between two arbitrary stream types.

The plugin mechanism is used everywhere in GStreamer, even if only the standard packages are being used. A few very basic functions reside in the core library, and all others are implemented in plugins. A plugin registry is used to store the details of the plugins in an binary registry file. This way, a program using GStreamer does not have to load all plugins to determine which are needed. Plugins are only loaded when their provided elements are requested.

See the *GStreamer Library Reference* for the current implementation details of GstElement (../../gstreamer/html/GstElement.html) and GstPlugin (../../gstreamer/html/GstPlugin.html).

2.2. Pads

Pads are used to negotiate links and data flow between elements in GStreamer. A pad can be viewed as a "place" or "port" on an element where links may be made with other elements, and through which data can flow to or from those elements. Pads have specific data handling capabilities: A pad can restrict the type of data that flows through it. Links are only allowed between two pads when the allowed data types of the two pads are compatible.

An analogy may be helpful here. A pad is similar to a plug or jack on a physical device. Consider, for example, a home theater system consisting of an amplifier, a DVD player, and a (silent) video projector. Linking the DVD player to the amplifier is allowed because both devices have audio jacks, and linking the projector to the DVD player is allowed because both devices have compatible video jacks. Links between the projector and the amplifier may not be made because the projector and amplifier have different types of jacks. Pads in GStreamer serve the same purpose as the jacks in the home theater system.

For the most part, all data in GStreamer flows one way through a link between elements. Data flows out of one element through one or more *source pads*, and elements accept incoming data through one or more *sink pads*. Source and sink elements have only source and sink pads, respectively.

See the *GStreamer Library Reference* for the current implementation details of a `GstPad` (../../gstreamer/html/GstPad.html).

2.3. GstMiniObject, Buffers and Events

All streams of data in GStreamer are chopped up into chunks that are passed from a source pad on one element to a sink pad on another element. *GstMiniObject* is the structure used to hold these chunks of data.

GstMiniObject contains the following important types:

- An exact type indicating what type of data (event, buffer, ...) this GstMiniObject is.
- A reference count indicating the number of elements currently holding a reference to the miniobject. When the reference count falls to zero, the miniobject will be disposed, and its memory will be freed in some sense (see below for more details).

For data transport, there are two types of GstMiniObject defined: events (control) and buffers (content).

Buffers may contain any sort of data that the two linked pads know how to handle. Normally, a buffer contains a chunk of some sort of audio or video data that flows from one element to another.

Buffers also contain metadata describing the buffer's contents. Some of the important types of metadata are:

- Pointers to one or more GstMemory objects. GstMemory objects are refcounted objects that encapsulate a region of memory.
- A timestamp indicating the preferred display timestamp of the content in the buffer.

Events contain information on the state of the stream flowing between the two linked pads. Events will only be sent if the element explicitly supports them, else the core will (try to) handle the events automatically. Events are used to indicate, for example, a media type, the end of a media stream or that the cache should be flushed.

Events may contain several of the following items:

- A subtype indicating the type of the contained event.
- The other contents of the event depend on the specific event type.

Events will be discussed extensively in Chapter 17. Until then, the only event that will be used is the *EOS* event, which is used to indicate the end-of-stream (usually end-of-file).

See the *GStreamer Library Reference* for the current implementation details of a `GstMiniObject` (../../gstreamer/html/gstreamer-GstMiniObject.html), `GstBuffer` (../../gstreamer/html/GstBuffer.html) and `GstEvent` (../../gstreamer/html/GstEvent.html).

2.3.1. Buffer Allocation

Buffers are able to store chunks of memory of several different types. The most generic type of buffer contains memory allocated by malloc(). Such buffers, although convenient, are not always very fast, since data often needs to be specifically copied into the buffer.

Many specialized elements create buffers that point to special memory. For example, the filesrc element usually maps a file into the address space of the application (using mmap()), and creates buffers that point into that address range. These buffers created by filesrc act exactly like generic buffers, except that they are read-only. The buffer freeing code automatically determines the correct method of freeing the underlying memory. Downstream elements that receive these kinds of buffers do not need to do anything special to handle or unreference it.

Another way an element might get specialized buffers is to request them from a downstream peer through a GstBufferPool or GstAllocator. Elements can ask a GstBufferPool or GstAllocator from the downstream peer element. If downstream is able to provide these objects, upstream can use them to allocate buffers. See more in Memory allocation.

Many sink elements have accelerated methods for copying data to hardware, or have direct access to hardware. It is common for these elements to be able to create a GstBufferPool or GstAllocator for their upstream peers. One such example is ximagesink. It creates buffers that contain XImages. Thus, when an upstream peer copies data into the buffer, it is copying directly into the XImage, enabling ximagesink to draw the image directly to the screen instead of having to copy data into an XImage first.

Filter elements often have the opportunity to either work on a buffer in-place, or work while copying from a source buffer to a destination buffer. It is optimal to implement both algorithms, since the GStreamer framework can choose the fastest algorithm as appropriate. Naturally, this only makes sense for strict filters -- elements that have exactly the same format on source and sink pads.

2.4. Media types and Properties

GStreamer uses a type system to ensure that the data passed between elements is in a recognized format. The type system is also important for ensuring that the parameters required to fully specify a format match up correctly when linking pads between elements. Each link that is made between elements has a specified type and optionally a set of properties. See more about caps negotiation in Caps negotiation.

2.4.1. The Basic Types

GStreamer already supports many basic media types. Following is a table of a few of the basic types used for buffers in GStreamer. The table contains the name ("media type") and a description of the type, the properties associated with the type, and the meaning of each property. A full list of supported types is included in List of Defined Types.

Table 2-1. Table of Example Types

Media Type	Description	Property	Property Type	Property Values	Property Description
audio/*	*All audio types*	rate	integer	greater than 0	The sample rate of the data, in samples (per channel) per second.
	channels	integer	greater than 0	The number of channels of audio data.	

Media Type	Description	Property	Property Type	Property Values	Property Description
audio/x-raw	Unstructured and uncompressed raw integer audio data.	format	string	S8 U8 S16LE S16BE U16LE U16BE S24_32LE S24_32BE U24_32LE U24_32BE S32LE S32BE U32LE U32BE S24LE S24BE U24LE U24BE S20LE S20BE U20LE U20BE S18LE S18BE U18LE U18BE F32LE F32BE F64LE F64BE	The format of the sample data.
audio/mpeg	Audio data compressed using the MPEG audio encoding scheme.	mpegversion	integer	1, 2 or 4	The MPEG-version used for encoding the data. The value 1 refers to MPEG-1, -2 and -2.5 layer 1, 2 or 3. The values 2 and 4 refer to the MPEG-AAC audio encoding schemes.
		framed	boolean	0 or 1	A true value indicates that each buffer contains exactly one frame. A false value indicates that frames and buffers do not necessarily match up.

Media Type	Description	Property	Property Type	Property Values	Property Description
layer	integer	1, 2, or 3	The compression scheme layer used to compress the data *(only if mpegversion=1)*.		
bitrate	integer	greater than 0	The bitrate, in bits per second. For VBR (variable bitrate) MPEG data, this is the average bitrate.		
audio/x-vorbis	Vorbis audio data				There are currently no specific properties defined for this type.

II. Building a Plugin

You are now ready to learn how to build a plugin. In this part of the guide, you will learn how to apply basic GStreamer programming concepts to write a simple plugin. The previous parts of the guide have contained no explicit example code, perhaps making things a bit abstract and difficult to understand. In contrast, this section will present both applications and code by following the development of an example audio filter plugin called "MyFilter".

The example filter element will begin with a single input pad and a single output pad. The filter will, at first, simply pass media and event data from its sink pad to its source pad without modification. But by the end of this part of the guide, you will learn to add some more interesting functionality, including properties and signal handlers. And after reading the next part of the guide, Advanced Filter Concepts, you will be able to add even more functionality to your plugins.

Chapter 3. Constructing the Boilerplate

In this chapter you will learn how to construct the bare minimum code for a new plugin. Starting from ground zero, you will see how to get the GStreamer template source. Then you will learn how to use a few basic tools to copy and modify a template plugin to create a new plugin. If you follow the examples here, then by the end of this chapter you will have a functional audio filter plugin that you can compile and use in GStreamer applications.

3.1. Getting the GStreamer Plugin Templates

There are currently two ways to develop a new plugin for GStreamer: You can write the entire plugin by hand, or you can copy an existing plugin template and write the plugin code you need. The second method is by far the simpler of the two, so the first method will not even be described here. (Errm, that is, "it is left as an exercise to the reader.")

The first step is to check out a copy of the `gst-template` git module to get an important tool and the source code template for a basic GStreamer plugin. To check out the `gst-template` module, make sure you are connected to the internet, and type the following commands at a command console:

```
shell $ git clone git://anongit.freedesktop.org/gstreamer/gst-template.git
Initialized empty Git repository in /some/path/gst-template/.git/
remote: Counting objects: 373, done.
remote: Compressing objects: 100% (114/114), done.
remote: Total 373 (delta 240), reused 373 (delta 240)
Receiving objects: 100% (373/373), 75.16 KiB | 78 KiB/s, done.
Resolving deltas: 100% (240/240), done.
```

This command will check out a series of files and directories into `gst-template`. The template you will be using is in the `gst-template/gst-plugin/` directory. You should look over the files in that directory to get a general idea of the structure of a source tree for a plugin.

If for some reason you can't access the git repository, you can also download a snapshot of the latest revision (http://cgit.freedesktop.org/gstreamer/gst-template/commit/) via the cgit web interface.

3.2. Using the Project Stamp

The first thing to do when making a new element is to specify some basic details about it: what its name is, who wrote it, what version number it is, etc. We also need to define an object to represent the element and to store the data the element needs. These details are collectively known as the *boilerplate*.

The standard way of defining the boilerplate is simply to write some code, and fill in some structures. As mentioned in the previous section, the easiest way to do this is to copy a template and add functionality according to your needs. To help you do so, there is a tool in the `./gst-plugin/tools/` directory. This tool, `make_element`, is a command line utility that creates the boilerplate code for you.

To use **make_element**, first open up a terminal window. Change to the `gst-template/gst-plugin/src` directory, and then run the **make_element** command. The arguments to the **make_element** are:

1. the name of the plugin, and

2. the source file that the tool will use. By default, `gstplugin` is used.

For example, the following commands create the MyFilter plugin based on the plugin template and put the output files in the `gst-template/gst-plugin/src` directory:

```
shell $ cd gst-template/gst-plugin/src
shell $ ../tools/make_element MyFilter
```

> **Note:** Capitalization is important for the name of the plugin. Keep in mind that under some operating systems, capitalization is also important when specifying directory and file names in general.

The last command creates two files: `gstmyfilter.c` and `gstmyfilter.h`.

> **Note:** It is recommended that you create a copy of the `gst-plugin` directory before continuing.

Now one needs to adjust the `Makefile.am` to use the new filenames and run `autogen.sh` from the parent directory to bootstrap the build environment. After that, the project can be built and installed using the well known **make && sudo make install** commands.

> **Note:** Be aware that by default `autogen.sh` and `configure` would choose `/usr/local` as a default location. One would need to add `/usr/local/lib/gstreamer-1.0` to GST_PLUGIN_PATH in order to make the new plugin show up in a gstreamer that's been installed from packages.

> **Note:** FIXME: this section is slightly outdated. gst-template is still useful as an example for a minimal plugin build system skeleton. However, for creating elements the tool gst-element-maker from gst-plugins-bad is recommended these days.

3.3. Examining the Basic Code

First we will examine the code you would be likely to place in a header file (although since the interface to the code is entirely defined by the plugin system, and doesn't depend on reading a header file, this is not crucial.)

Example 3-1. Example Plugin Header File

```
#include <gst/gst.h>

/* Definition of structure storing data for this element. */
typedef struct _GstMyFilter {
  GstElement element;

  GstPad *sinkpad, *srcpad;

  gboolean silent;



} GstMyFilter;

/* Standard definition defining a class for this element. */
typedef struct _GstMyFilterClass {
  GstElementClass parent_class;
} GstMyFilterClass;

/* Standard macros for defining types for this element.  */
#define GST_TYPE_MY_FILTER (gst_my_filter_get_type())
#define GST_MY_FILTER(obj) \
  (G_TYPE_CHECK_INSTANCE_CAST((obj),GST_TYPE_MY_FILTER,GstMyFilter))
#define GST_MY_FILTER_CLASS(klass) \
  (G_TYPE_CHECK_CLASS_CAST((klass),GST_TYPE_MY_FILTER,GstMyFilterClass))
#define GST_IS_MY_FILTER(obj) \
  (G_TYPE_CHECK_INSTANCE_TYPE((obj),GST_TYPE_MY_FILTER))
#define GST_IS_MY_FILTER_CLASS(klass) \
  (G_TYPE_CHECK_CLASS_TYPE((klass),GST_TYPE_MY_FILTER))

/* Standard function returning type information. */
GType gst_my_filter_get_type (void);
```

Using this header file, you can use the following macro to setup the `GObject` basics in your source file so that all functions will be called appropriately:

```
#include "filter.h"

G_DEFINE_TYPE (GstMyFilter, gst_my_filter, GST_TYPE_ELEMENT);
```

3.4. Element metadata

The Element metadata provides extra element information. It is configured with `gst_element_class_set_metadata` or `gst_element_class_set_static_metadata` which takes the following parameters:

- A long, English, name for the element.

- The type of the element, see the docs/design/draft-klass.txt document in the GStreamer core source tree for details and examples.

- A brief description of the purpose of the element.

- The name of the author of the element, optionally followed by a contact email address in angle brackets.

For example:

```
gst_element_class_set_static_metadata (klass,
  "An example plugin",
  "Example/FirstExample",
  "Shows the basic structure of a plugin",
  "your name <your.name@your.isp>");
```

The element details are registered with the plugin during the `_class_init ()` function, which is part of the GObject system. The `_class_init ()` function should be set for this GObject in the function where you register the type with GLib.

```
static void
gst_my_filter_class_init (GstMyFilterClass * klass)
{
  GstElementClass *element_class = GST_ELEMENT_CLASS (klass);

[..]
  gst_element_class_set_static_metadata (element_klass,
    "An example plugin",
    "Example/FirstExample",
    "Shows the basic structure of a plugin",
    "your name <your.name@your.isp>");

}
```

3.5. GstStaticPadTemplate

A GstStaticPadTemplate is a description of a pad that the element will (or might) create and use. It contains:

- A short name for the pad.

- Pad direction.

- Existence property. This indicates whether the pad exists always (an "always" pad), only in some cases (a "sometimes" pad) or only if the application requested such a pad (a "request" pad).

- Supported types by this element (capabilities).

For example:

```
static GstStaticPadTemplate sink_factory =
GST_STATIC_PAD_TEMPLATE (
  "sink",
  GST_PAD_SINK,
  GST_PAD_ALWAYS,
  GST_STATIC_CAPS ("ANY")
);
```

Those pad templates are registered during the `_class_init ()` function with the `gst_element_class_add_pad_template ()`. For this function you need a handle the `GstPadTemplate` which you can create from the static pad template with `gst_static_pad_template_get ()`. See below for more details on this.

Pads are created from these static templates in the element's `_init ()` function using `gst_pad_new_from_static_template ()`. In order to create a new pad from this template using `gst_pad_new_from_static_template ()`, you will need to declare the pad template as a global variable. More on this subject in Chapter 4.

```
static GstStaticPadTemplate sink_factory = [..],
    src_factory = [..];

static void
gst_my_filter_class_init (GstMyFilterClass * klass)
{
  GstElementClass *element_class = GST_ELEMENT_CLASS (klass);
[..]

  gst_element_class_add_pad_template (element_class,
gst_static_pad_template_get (&src_factory));
  gst_element_class_add_pad_template (element_class,
gst_static_pad_template_get (&sink_factory));
}
```

The last argument in a template is its type or list of supported types. In this example, we use 'ANY', which means that this element will accept all input. In real-life situations, you would set a media type and optionally a set of properties to make sure that only supported input will come in. This representation should be a string that starts with a media type, then a set of comma-separates properties with their supported values. In case of an audio filter that supports raw integer 16-bit audio, mono or stereo at any samplerate, the correct template would look like this:

```
static GstStaticPadTemplate sink_factory =
GST_STATIC_PAD_TEMPLATE (
  "sink",
  GST_PAD_SINK,
  GST_PAD_ALWAYS,
  GST_STATIC_CAPS (
    "audio/x-raw, "
      "format = (string) " GST_AUDIO_NE (S16) ", "
      "channels = (int) { 1, 2 }, "
      "rate = (int) [ 8000, 96000 ]"
  )
);
```

Values surrounded by curly brackets ("{" and "}") are lists, values surrounded by square brackets ("[" and "]") are ranges. Multiple sets of types are supported too, and should be separated by a semicolon (";"). Later, in the chapter on pads, we will see how to use types to know the exact format of a stream: Chapter 4.

3.6. Constructor Functions

Each element has two functions which are used for construction of an element. The _class_init() function, which is used to initialise the class only once (specifying what signals, arguments and virtual functions the class has and setting up global state); and the _init() function, which is used to initialise a specific instance of this type.

3.7. The plugin_init function

Once we have written code defining all the parts of the plugin, we need to write the plugin_init() function. This is a special function, which is called as soon as the plugin is loaded, and should return TRUE or FALSE depending on whether it loaded initialized any dependencies correctly. Also, in this function, any supported element type in the plugin should be registered.

```
static gboolean
plugin_init (GstPlugin *plugin)
{
```

```
    return gst_element_register (plugin, "my_filter",
        GST_RANK_NONE,
        GST_TYPE_MY_FILTER);
}

GST_PLUGIN_DEFINE (
  GST_VERSION_MAJOR,
  GST_VERSION_MINOR,
  my_filter,
  "My filter plugin",
  plugin_init,
  VERSION,
  "LGPL",
  "GStreamer",
  "http://gstreamer.net/"
)
```

Note that the information returned by the plugin_init() function will be cached in a central registry. For this reason, it is important that the same information is always returned by the function: for example, it must not make element factories available based on runtime conditions. If an element can only work in certain conditions (for example, if the soundcard is not being used by some other process) this must be reflected by the element being unable to enter the READY state if unavailable, rather than the plugin attempting to deny existence of the plugin.

Chapter 4. Specifying the pads

As explained before, pads are the port through which data goes in and out of your element, and that makes them a very important item in the process of element creation. In the boilerplate code, we have seen how static pad templates take care of registering pad templates with the element class. Here, we will see how to create actual elements, use an _event () -function to configure for a particular format and how to register functions to let data flow through the element.

In the element _init () function, you create the pad from the pad template that has been registered with the element class in the _class_init () function. After creating the pad, you have to set a _chain () function pointer that will receive and process the input data on the sinkpad. You can optionally also set an _event () function pointer and a _query () function pointer. Alternatively, pads can also operate in looping mode, which means that they can pull data themselves. More on this topic later. After that, you have to register the pad with the element. This happens like this:

```
static void
gst_my_filter_init (GstMyFilter *filter)
{
  /* pad through which data comes in to the element */
  filter->sinkpad = gst_pad_new_from_static_template (
&sink_template, "sink");
  /* pads are configured here with gst_pad_set_*_function () */



  gst_element_add_pad (GST_ELEMENT (filter), filter->sinkpad);

  /* pad through which data goes out of the element */
  filter->srcpad = gst_pad_new_from_static_template (
&src_template, "src");
  /* pads are configured here with gst_pad_set_*_function () */



  gst_element_add_pad (GST_ELEMENT (filter), filter->srcpad);

  /* properties initial value */
  filter->silent = FALSE;
}
```

Chapter 5. The chain function

The chain function is the function in which all data processing takes place. In the case of a simple filter, _chain () functions are mostly linear functions - so for each incoming buffer, one buffer will go out, too. Below is a very simple implementation of a chain function:

```
static GstFlowReturn gst_my_filter_chain (GstPad    *pad,
                                           GstObject *parent,
                                           GstBuffer *buf);

[..]

static void
gst_my_filter_init (GstMyFilter * filter)
{
[..]
  /* configure chain function on the pad before adding
   * the pad to the element */
  gst_pad_set_chain_function (filter->sinkpad,
      gst_my_filter_chain);
[..]
}

static GstFlowReturn
gst_my_filter_chain (GstPad    *pad,
                     GstObject *parent,
    GstBuffer *buf)
{
  GstMyFilter *filter = GST_MY_FILTER (parent);

  if (!filter->silent)
    g_print ("Have data of size %" G_GSIZE_FORMAT" bytes!\n",
        gst_buffer_get_size (buf));

  return gst_pad_push (filter->srcpad, buf);
}
```

Obviously, the above doesn't do much useful. Instead of printing that the data is in, you would normally process the data there. Remember, however, that buffers are not always writeable.

In more advanced elements (the ones that do event processing), you may want to additionally specify an event handling function, which will be called when stream-events are sent (such as caps, end-of-stream, newsegment, tags, etc.).

```
static void
gst_my_filter_init (GstMyFilter * filter)
{
```

```
[..]
  gst_pad_set_event_function (filter->sinkpad,
      gst_my_filter_sink_event);
[..]
}



static gboolean
gst_my_filter_sink_event (GstPad     *pad,
          GstObject *parent,
          GstEvent  *event)
{
  GstMyFilter *filter = GST_MY_FILTER (parent);

  switch (GST_EVENT_TYPE (event)) {
    case GST_EVENT_CAPS:
      /* we should handle the format here */
      break;
    case GST_EVENT_EOS:
      /* end-of-stream, we should close down all stream leftovers here */
      gst_my_filter_stop_processing (filter);
      break;
    default:
      break;
  }

  return gst_pad_event_default (pad, parent, event);
}

static GstFlowReturn
gst_my_filter_chain (GstPad     *pad,
    GstObject *parent,
    GstBuffer *buf)
{
  GstMyFilter *filter = GST_MY_FILTER (parent);
  GstBuffer *outbuf;

  outbuf = gst_my_filter_process_data (filter, buf);
  gst_buffer_unref (buf);
  if (!outbuf) {
    /* something went wrong - signal an error */
    GST_ELEMENT_ERROR (GST_ELEMENT (filter), STREAM, FAILED, (NULL), (NULL));
    return GST_FLOW_ERROR;
  }

  return gst_pad_push (filter->srcpad, outbuf);
}
```

In some cases, it might be useful for an element to have control over the input data rate, too. In that case, you probably want to write a so-called *loop-based* element. Source elements (with only source pads) can also be *get-based* elements. These concepts will be explained in the advanced section of this guide, and in the section that specifically discusses source pads.

Chapter 6. The event function

The event function notifies you of special events that happen in the datastream (such as caps, end-of-stream, newsegment, tags, etc.). Events can travel both upstream and downstream, so you can receive them on sink pads as well as source pads.

Below follows a very simple event function that we install on the sink pad of our element.

```
static gboolean gst_my_filter_sink_event (GstPad     *pad,
                                           GstObject *parent,
                                           GstEvent  *event);

[..]

static void
gst_my_filter_init (GstMyFilter * filter)
{
[..]
  /* configure event function on the pad before adding
   * the pad to the element */
  gst_pad_set_event_function (filter->sinkpad,
      gst_my_filter_sink_event);
[..]
}

static gboolean
gst_my_filter_sink_event (GstPad     *pad,
        GstObject *parent,
        GstEvent  *event)
{
  gboolean ret;
  GstMyFilter *filter = GST_MY_FILTER (parent);

  switch (GST_EVENT_TYPE (event)) {
    case GST_EVENT_CAPS:
      /* we should handle the format here */

      /* push the event downstream */
      ret = gst_pad_push_event (filter->srcpad, event);
      break;
    case GST_EVENT_EOS:
      /* end-of-stream, we should close down all stream leftovers here */
      gst_my_filter_stop_processing (filter);

      ret = gst_pad_event_default (pad, parent, event);
      break;
    default:
      /* just call the default handler */
      ret = gst_pad_event_default (pad, parent, event);
```

```
      break;
  }
  return ret;
}
```

It is a good idea to call the default event handler `gst_pad_event_default ()` for unknown events. Depending on the event type, the default handler will forward the event or simply unref it. The CAPS event is by default not forwarded so we need to do this in the event handler ourselves.

Chapter 7. The query function

Through the query function, your element will receive queries that it has to reply to. These are queries like position, duration but also about the supported formats and scheduling modes your element supports. Queries can travel both upstream and downstream, so you can receive them on sink pads as well as source pads.

Below follows a very simple query function that we install on the source pad of our element.

```
static gboolean gst_my_filter_src_query (GstPad     *pad,
                                          GstObject *parent,
                                          GstQuery  *query);

[..]

static void
gst_my_filter_init (GstMyFilter * filter)
{
[..]
  /* configure event function on the pad before adding
   * the pad to the element */
  gst_pad_set_query_function (filter->srcpad,
      gst_my_filter_src_query);
[..]
}

static gboolean
gst_my_filter_src_query (GstPad     *pad,
        GstObject *parent,
        GstQuery  *query)
{
  gboolean ret;
  GstMyFilter *filter = GST_MY_FILTER (parent);

  switch (GST_QUERY_TYPE (query)) {
    case GST_QUERY_POSITION:
      /* we should report the current position */
      [...]
      break;
    case GST_QUERY_DURATION:
      /* we should report the duration here */
      [...]
      break;
    case GST_QUERY_CAPS:
      /* we should report the supported caps here */
      [...]
      break;
    default:
      /* just call the default handler */
```

```
        ret = gst_pad_query_default (pad, parent, query);
        break;
  }
  return ret;
}
```

It is a good idea to call the default query handler `gst_pad_query_default ()` for unknown queries. Depending on the query type, the default handler will forward the query or simply unref it.

Chapter 8. What are states?

A state describes whether the element instance is initialized, whether it is ready to transfer data and whether it is currently handling data. There are four states defined in GStreamer:

- GST_STATE_NULL

- GST_STATE_READY

- GST_STATE_PAUSED

- GST_STATE_PLAYING

which will from now on be referred to simply as "NULL", "READY", "PAUSED" and "PLAYING".

GST_STATE_NULL is the default state of an element. In this state, it has not allocated any runtime resources, it has not loaded any runtime libraries and it can obviously not handle data.

GST_STATE_READY is the next state that an element can be in. In the READY state, an element has all default resources (runtime-libraries, runtime-memory) allocated. However, it has not yet allocated or defined anything that is stream-specific. When going from NULL to READY state (GST_STATE_CHANGE_NULL_TO_READY), an element should allocate any non-stream-specific resources and should load runtime-loadable libraries (if any). When going the other way around (from READY to NULL, GST_STATE_CHANGE_READY_TO_NULL), an element should unload these libraries and free all allocated resources. Examples of such resources are hardware devices. Note that files are generally streams, and these should thus be considered as stream-specific resources; therefore, they should *not* be allocated in this state.

GST_STATE_PAUSED is the state in which an element is ready to accept and handle data. For most elements this state is the same as PLAYING. The only exception to this rule are sink elements. Sink elements only accept one single buffer of data and then block. At this point the pipeline is 'prerolled' and ready to render data immediately.

GST_STATE_PLAYING is the highest state that an element can be in. For most elements this state is exactly the same as PAUSED, they accept and process events and buffers with data. Only sink elements need to differentiate between PAUSED and PLAYING state. In PLAYING state, sink elements actually render incoming data, e.g. output audio to a sound card or render video pictures to an image sink.

8.1. Managing filter state

If at all possible, your element should derive from one of the new base classes (Pre-made base classes). There are ready-made general purpose base classes for different types of sources, sinks and filter/transformation elements. In addition to those, specialised base classes exist for audio and video elements and others.

If you use a base class, you will rarely have to handle state changes yourself. All you have to do is override the base class's start() and stop() virtual functions (might be called differently depending on the base class) and the base class will take care of everything for you.

If, however, you do not derive from a ready-made base class, but from GstElement or some other class not built on top of a base class, you will most likely have to implement your own state change function to be notified of state changes. This is definitely necessary if your plugin is a demuxer or a muxer, as there are no base classes for muxers or demuxers yet.

An element can be notified of state changes through a virtual function pointer. Inside this function, the element can initialize any sort of specific data needed by the element, and it can optionally fail to go from one state to another.

Do not g_assert for unhandled state changes; this is taken care of by the GstElement base class.

```
static GstStateChangeReturn
gst_my_filter_change_state (GstElement *element, GstStateChange transition);

static void
gst_my_filter_class_init (GstMyFilterClass *klass)
{
  GstElementClass *element_class = GST_ELEMENT_CLASS (klass);

  element_class->change_state = gst_my_filter_change_state;
}



static GstStateChangeReturn
gst_my_filter_change_state (GstElement *element, GstStateChange transition)
{
  GstStateChangeReturn ret = GST_STATE_CHANGE_SUCCESS;
  GstMyFilter *filter = GST_MY_FILTER (element);

  switch (transition) {
    case GST_STATE_CHANGE_NULL_TO_READY:
      if (!gst_my_filter_allocate_memory (filter))
        return GST_STATE_CHANGE_FAILURE;
      break;
    default:
      break;
  }

  ret = GST_ELEMENT_CLASS (parent_class)->change_state (element, transition);
  if (ret == GST_STATE_CHANGE_FAILURE)
    return ret;

  switch (transition) {
    case GST_STATE_CHANGE_READY_TO_NULL:
      gst_my_filter_free_memory (filter);
```

```
      break;
    default:
      break;
  }

  return ret;
}
```

Note that upwards (NULL=>READY, READY=>PAUSED, PAUSED=>PLAYING) and downwards (PLAYING=>PAUSED, PAUSED=>READY, READY=>NULL) state changes are handled in two separate blocks with the downwards state change handled only after we have chained up to the parent class's state change function. This is necessary in order to safely handle concurrent access by multiple threads.

The reason for this is that in the case of downwards state changes you don't want to destroy allocated resources while your plugin's chain function (for example) is still accessing those resources in another thread. Whether your chain function might be running or not depends on the state of your plugin's pads, and the state of those pads is closely linked to the state of the element. Pad states are handled in the GstElement class's state change function, including proper locking, that's why it is essential to chain up before destroying allocated resources.

Chapter 9. Adding Properties

The primary and most important way of controlling how an element behaves, is through GObject properties. GObject properties are defined in the _class_init () function. The element optionally implements a _get_property () and a _set_property () function. These functions will be notified if an application changes or requests the value of a property, and can then fill in the value or take action required for that property to change value internally.

You probably also want to keep an instance variable around with the currently configured value of the property that you use in the get and set functions. Note that GObject will not automatically set your instance variable to the default value, you will have to do that in the _init () function of your element.

```
/* properties */
enum {
  PROP_0,
  PROP_SILENT
  /* FILL ME */
};

static void gst_my_filter_set_property (GObject        *object,
 guint          prop_id,
 const GValue *value,
 GParamSpec   *pspec);
static void gst_my_filter_get_property (GObject        *object,
 guint          prop_id,
 GValue         *value,
 GParamSpec   *pspec);

static void
gst_my_filter_class_init (GstMyFilterClass *klass)
{
  GObjectClass *object_class = G_OBJECT_CLASS (klass);

  /* define virtual function pointers */
  object_class->set_property = gst_my_filter_set_property;
  object_class->get_property = gst_my_filter_get_property;

  /* define properties */
  g_object_class_install_property (object_class, PROP_SILENT,
    g_param_spec_boolean ("silent", "Silent",
  "Whether to be very verbose or not",
  FALSE, G_PARAM_READWRITE | G_PARAM_STATIC_STRINGS));
}

static void
gst_my_filter_set_property (GObject        *object,
    guint          prop_id,
    const GValue *value,
    GParamSpec   *pspec)
```

```
{
  GstMyFilter *filter = GST_MY_FILTER (object);

  switch (prop_id) {
    case PROP_SILENT:
      filter->silent = g_value_get_boolean (value);
      g_print ("Silent argument was changed to %s\n",
       filter->silent ? "true" : "false");
      break;
    default:
      G_OBJECT_WARN_INVALID_PROPERTY_ID (object, prop_id, pspec);
      break;
  }
}

static void
gst_my_filter_get_property (GObject      *object,
    guint         prop_id,
    GValue       *value,
    GParamSpec *pspec)
{
  GstMyFilter *filter = GST_MY_FILTER (object);

  switch (prop_id) {
    case PROP_SILENT:
      g_value_set_boolean (value, filter->silent);
      break;
    default:
      G_OBJECT_WARN_INVALID_PROPERTY_ID (object, prop_id, pspec);
      break;
  }
}
```

The above is a very simple example of how properties are used. Graphical applications will use these properties and will display a user-controllable widget with which these properties can be changed. This means that - for the property to be as user-friendly as possible - you should be as exact as possible in the definition of the property. Not only in defining ranges in between which valid properties can be located (for integers, floats, etc.), but also in using very descriptive (better yet: internationalized) strings in the definition of the property, and if possible using enums and flags instead of integers. The GObject documentation describes these in a very complete way, but below, we'll give a short example of where this is useful. Note that using integers here would probably completely confuse the user, because they make no sense in this context. The example is stolen from videotestsrc.

```
typedef enum {
  GST_VIDEOTESTSRC_SMPTE,
  GST_VIDEOTESTSRC_SNOW,
  GST_VIDEOTESTSRC_BLACK
} GstVideotestsrcPattern;

[..]
```

```
#define GST_TYPE_VIDEOTESTSRC_PATTERN (gst_videotestsrc_pattern_get_type ())
static GType
gst_videotestsrc_pattern_get_type (void)
{
  static GType videotestsrc_pattern_type = 0;

  if (!videotestsrc_pattern_type) {
    static GEnumValue pattern_types[] = {
      { GST_VIDEOTESTSRC_SMPTE, "SMPTE 100% color bars",   "smpte" },
      { GST_VIDEOTESTSRC_SNOW,  "Random (television snow)", "snow"  },
      { GST_VIDEOTESTSRC_BLACK, "0% Black",                "black" },
      { 0, NULL, NULL },
    };

    videotestsrc_pattern_type =
g_enum_register_static ("GstVideotestsrcPattern",
pattern_types);
  }

  return videotestsrc_pattern_type;
}

[..]

static void
gst_videotestsrc_class_init (GstvideotestsrcClass *klass)
{
[..]
  g_object_class_install_property (G_OBJECT_CLASS (klass), PROP_PATTERN,
    g_param_spec_enum ("pattern", "Pattern",
      "Type of test pattern to generate",
                  GST_TYPE_VIDEOTESTSRC_PATTERN, GST_VIDEOTESTSRC_SMPTE,
                  G_PARAM_READWRITE | G_PARAM_STATIC_STRINGS));
[..]
}
```

Chapter 10. Signals

GObject signals can be used to notify applications of events specific to this object. Note, however, that the application needs to be aware of signals and their meaning, so if you're looking for a generic way for application-element interaction, signals are probably not what you're looking for. In many cases, however, signals can be very useful. See the GObject documentation (http://library.gnome.org/devel/gobject/stable/) for all internals about signals.

Chapter 11. Building a Test Application

Often, you will want to test your newly written plugin in an as small setting as possible. Usually, `gst-launch-1.0` is a good first step at testing a plugin. If you have not installed your plugin in a directory that GStreamer searches, then you will need to set the plugin path. Either set GST_PLUGIN_PATH to the directory containing your plugin, or use the command-line option --gst-plugin-path. If you based your plugin off of the gst-plugin template, then this will look something like **gst-launch-1.0 --gst-plugin-path=$HOME/gst-template/gst-plugin/src/.libs TESTPIPELINE** However, you will often need more testing features than gst-launch-1.0 can provide, such as seeking, events, interactivity and more. Writing your own small testing program is the easiest way to accomplish this. This section explains - in a few words - how to do that. For a complete application development guide, see the Application Development Manual (../../manual/html/index.html).

At the start, you need to initialize the GStreamer core library by calling `gst_init ()`. You can alternatively call `gst_init_get_option_group ()`, which will return a pointer to GOptionGroup. You can then use GOption to handle the initialization, and this will finish the GStreamer initialization.

You can create elements using `gst_element_factory_make ()`, where the first argument is the element type that you want to create, and the second argument is a free-form name. The example at the end uses a simple filesource - decoder - soundcard output pipeline, but you can use specific debugging elements if that's necessary. For example, an `identity` element can be used in the middle of the pipeline to act as a data-to-application transmitter. This can be used to check the data for misbehaviours or correctness in your test application. Also, you can use a `fakesink` element at the end of the pipeline to dump your data to the stdout (in order to do this, set the `dump` property to TRUE). Lastly, you can use valgrind to check for memory errors.

During linking, your test application can use filtered caps as a way to drive a specific type of data to or from your element. This is a very simple and effective way of checking multiple types of input and output in your element.

Note that during running, you should listen for at least the "error" and "eos" messages on the bus and/or your plugin/element to check for correct handling of this. Also, you should add events into the pipeline and make sure your plugin handles these correctly (with respect to clocking, internal caching, etc.).

Never forget to clean up memory in your plugin or your test application. When going to the NULL state, your element should clean up allocated memory and caches. Also, it should close down any references held to possible support libraries. Your application should `unref ()` the pipeline and make sure it doesn't crash.

```
#include <gst/gst.h>

static gboolean
bus_call (GstBus      *bus,
  GstMessage *msg,
```

```
    gpointer    data)
{
  GMainLoop *loop = data;

  switch (GST_MESSAGE_TYPE (msg)) {
    case GST_MESSAGE_EOS:
      g_print ("End-of-stream\n");
      g_main_loop_quit (loop);
      break;
    case GST_MESSAGE_ERROR: {
      gchar *debug = NULL;
      GError *err = NULL;

      gst_message_parse_error (msg, &err, &debug);

      g_print ("Error: %s\n", err->message);
      g_error_free (err);

      if (debug) {
        g_print ("Debug details: %s\n", debug);
        g_free (debug);
      }

      g_main_loop_quit (loop);
      break;
    }
    default:
      break;
  }

  return TRUE;
}

gint
main (gint    argc,
      gchar *argv[])
{
  GstStateChangeReturn ret;
  GstElement *pipeline, *filesrc, *decoder, *filter, *sink;
  GstElement *convert1, *convert2, *resample;
  GMainLoop *loop;
  GstBus *bus;
  guint watch_id;

  /* initialization */
  gst_init (&argc, &argv);
  loop = g_main_loop_new (NULL, FALSE);
  if (argc != 2) {
    g_print ("Usage: %s <mp3 filename>\n", argv[0]);
    return 01;
  }

  /* create elements */
```

```
pipeline = gst_pipeline_new ("my_pipeline");

/* watch for messages on the pipeline's bus (note that this will only
 * work like this when a GLib main loop is running) */
bus = gst_pipeline_get_bus (GST_PIPELINE (pipeline));
watch_id = gst_bus_add_watch (bus, bus_call, loop);
gst_object_unref (bus);

filesrc  = gst_element_factory_make ("filesrc", "my_filesource");
decoder  = gst_element_factory_make ("mad", "my_decoder");

/* putting an audioconvert element here to convert the output of the
 * decoder into a format that my_filter can handle (we are assuming it
 * will handle any sample rate here though) */
convert1 = gst_element_factory_make ("audioconvert", "audioconvert1");

/* use "identity" here for a filter that does nothing */
filter   = gst_element_factory_make ("my_filter", "my_filter");

/* there should always be audioconvert and audioresample elements before
 * the audio sink, since the capabilities of the audio sink usually vary
 * depending on the environment (output used, sound card, driver etc.) */
convert2 = gst_element_factory_make ("audioconvert", "audioconvert2");
resample = gst_element_factory_make ("audioresample", "audioresample");
sink     = gst_element_factory_make ("pulsesink", "audiosink");

if (!sink || !decoder) {
  g_print ("Decoder or output could not be found - check your install\n");
  return -1;
} else if (!convert1 || !convert2 || !resample) {
  g_print ("Could not create audioconvert or audioresample element, "
           "check your installation\n");
  return -1;
} else if (!filter) {
  g_print ("Your self-written filter could not be found. Make sure it "
           "is installed correctly in $(libdir)/gstreamer-1.0/ or "
           "~/.gstreamer-1.0/plugins/ and that gst-inspect-1.0 lists it. "
           "If it doesn't, check with 'GST_DEBUG=*:2 gst-inspect-1.0' for "
           "the reason why it is not being loaded.");
  return -1;
}

g_object_set (G_OBJECT (filesrc), "location", argv[1], NULL);

gst_bin_add_many (GST_BIN (pipeline), filesrc, decoder, convert1, filter,
                  convert2, resample, sink, NULL);

/* link everything together */
if (!gst_element_link_many (filesrc, decoder, convert1, filter, convert2,
                            resample, sink, NULL)) {
  g_print ("Failed to link one or more elements!\n");
  return -1;
}
```

```
  /* run */
  ret = gst_element_set_state (pipeline, GST_STATE_PLAYING);
  if (ret == GST_STATE_CHANGE_FAILURE) {
    GstMessage *msg;

    g_print ("Failed to start up pipeline!\n");

    /* check if there is an error message with details on the bus */
    msg = gst_bus_poll (bus, GST_MESSAGE_ERROR, 0);
    if (msg) {
      GError *err = NULL;

      gst_message_parse_error (msg, &err, NULL);
      g_print ("ERROR: %s\n", err->message);
      g_error_free (err);
      gst_message_unref (msg);
    }
    return -1;
  }

  g_main_loop_run (loop);

  /* clean up */
  gst_element_set_state (pipeline, GST_STATE_NULL);
  gst_object_unref (pipeline);
  g_source_remove (watch_id);
  g_main_loop_unref (loop);

  return 0;
}
```

III. Advanced Filter Concepts

By now, you should be able to create basic filter elements that can receive and send data. This is the simple model that GStreamer stands for. But GStreamer can do much more than only this! In this chapter, various advanced topics will be discussed, such as scheduling, special pad types, clocking, events, interfaces, tagging and more. These topics are the sugar that makes GStreamer so easy to use for applications.

Chapter 12. Request and Sometimes pads

Until now, we've only dealt with pads that are always available. However, there's also pads that are only being created in some cases, or only if the application requests the pad. The first is called a *sometimes*; the second is called a *request* pad. The availability of a pad (always, sometimes or request) can be seen in a pad's template. This chapter will discuss when each of the two is useful, how they are created and when they should be disposed.

12.1. Sometimes pads

A "sometimes" pad is a pad that is created under certain conditions, but not in all cases. This mostly depends on stream content: demuxers will generally parse the stream header, decide what elementary (video, audio, subtitle, etc.) streams are embedded inside the system stream, and will then create a sometimes pad for each of those elementary streams. At its own choice, it can also create more than one instance of each of those per element instance. The only limitation is that each newly created pad should have a unique name. Sometimes pads are disposed when the stream data is disposed, too (i.e. when going from PAUSED to the READY state). You should *not* dispose the pad on EOS, because someone might re-activate the pipeline and seek back to before the end-of-stream point. The stream should still stay valid after EOS, at least until the stream data is disposed. In any case, the element is always the owner of such a pad.

The example code below will parse a text file, where the first line is a number (n). The next lines all start with a number (0 to n-1), which is the number of the source pad over which the data should be sent.

```
3
0: foo
1: bar
0: boo
2: bye
```

The code to parse this file and create the dynamic "sometimes" pads, looks like this:

```
typedef struct _GstMyFilter {
[..]
  gboolean firstrun;
  GList *srcpadlist;
} GstMyFilter;

static GstStaticPadTemplate src_factory =
GST_STATIC_PAD_TEMPLATE (
  "src_%u",
  GST_PAD_SRC,
  GST_PAD_SOMETIMES,
  GST_STATIC_CAPS ("ANY")
```

```
);

static void
gst_my_filter_class_init (GstMyFilterClass *klass)
{
  GstElementClass *element_class = GST_ELEMENT_CLASS (klass);
[..]
  gst_element_class_add_pad_template (element_class,
gst_static_pad_template_get (&src_factory));
[..]
}

static void
gst_my_filter_init (GstMyFilter *filter)
{
[..]
  filter->firstrun = TRUE;
  filter->srcpadlist = NULL;
}

/*
 * Get one line of data - without newline.
 */

static GstBuffer *
gst_my_filter_getline (GstMyFilter *filter)
{
  guint8 *data;
  gint n, num;

  /* max. line length is 512 characters - for safety */
  for (n = 0; n < 512; n++) {
    num = gst_bytestream_peek_bytes (filter->bs, &data, n + 1);
    if (num != n + 1)
      return NULL;

    /* newline? */
    if (data[n] == '\n') {
      GstBuffer *buf = gst_buffer_new_allocate (NULL, n + 1, NULL);

      gst_bytestream_peek_bytes (filter->bs, &data, n);
      gst_buffer_fill (buf, 0, data, n);
      gst_buffer_memset (buf, n, '\0', 1);
      gst_bytestream_flush_fast (filter->bs, n + 1);

      return buf;
    }
  }
}

static void
gst_my_filter_loopfunc (GstElement *element)
{
```

```
GstMyFilter *filter = GST_MY_FILTER (element);
GstBuffer *buf;
GstPad *pad;
GstMapInfo map;
gint num, n;

/* parse header */
if (filter->firstrun) {
  gchar *padname;
  guint8 id;

  if (!(buf = gst_my_filter_getline (filter))) {
    gst_element_error (element, STREAM, READ, (NULL),
("Stream contains no header"));
    return;
  }
  gst_buffer_extract (buf, 0, &id, 1);
  num = atoi (id);
  gst_buffer_unref (buf);

  /* for each of the streams, create a pad */
  for (n = 0; n < num; n++) {
    padname = g_strdup_printf ("src_%u", n);
    pad = gst_pad_new_from_static_template (src_factory, padname);
    g_free (padname);

    /* here, you would set _event () and _query () functions */

    /* need to activate the pad before adding */
    gst_pad_set_active (pad, TRUE);

    gst_element_add_pad (element, pad);
    filter->srcpadlist = g_list_append (filter->srcpadlist, pad);
  }
}

/* and now, simply parse each line and push over */
if (!(buf = gst_my_filter_getline (filter))) {
  GstEvent *event = gst_event_new (GST_EVENT_EOS);
  GList *padlist;

  for (padlist = srcpadlist;
       padlist != NULL; padlist = g_list_next (padlist)) {
    pad = GST_PAD (padlist->data);
    gst_pad_push_event (pad, gst_event_ref (event));
  }
  gst_event_unref (event);
  /* pause the task here */
  return;
}

/* parse stream number and go beyond the ':' in the data */
gst_buffer_map (buf, &map, GST_MAP_READ);
```

```
    num = atoi (map.data[0]);
    if (num >= 0 && num < g_list_length (filter->srcpadlist)) {
      pad = GST_PAD (g_list_nth_data (filter->srcpadlist, num);

      /* magic buffer parsing foo */
      for (n = 0; map.data[n] != ':' &&
                  map.data[n] != '\0'; n++) ;
      if (map.data[n] != '\0') {
        GstBuffer *sub;

        /* create region copy that starts right past the space. The reason
         * that we don't just forward the data pointer is because the
         * pointer is no longer the start of an allocated block of memory,
         * but just a pointer to a position somewhere in the middle of it.
         * That cannot be freed upon disposal, so we'd either crash or have
         * a memleak. Creating a region copy is a simple way to solve that. */
        sub = gst_buffer_copy_region (buf, GST_BUFFER_COPY_ALL,
            n + 1, map.size - n - 1);
        gst_pad_push (pad, sub);
      }
    }
    gst_buffer_unmap (buf, &map);
    gst_buffer_unref (buf);
}
```

Note that we use a lot of checks everywhere to make sure that the content in the file is valid. This has two purposes: first, the file could be erroneous, in which case we prevent a crash. The second and most important reason is that - in extreme cases - the file could be used maliciously to cause undefined behaviour in the plugin, which might lead to security issues. *Always* assume that the file could be used to do bad things.

12.2. Request pads

"Request" pads are similar to sometimes pads, except that request are created on demand of something outside of the element rather than something inside the element. This concept is often used in muxers, where - for each elementary stream that is to be placed in the output system stream - one sink pad will be requested. It can also be used in elements with a variable number of input or outputs pads, such as the tee (multi-output) or input-selector (multi-input) elements.

To implement request pads, you need to provide a padtemplate with a GST_PAD_REQUEST presence and implement the request_new_pad virtual method in GstElement. To clean up, you will need to implement the release_pad virtual method.

```
static GstPad * gst_my_filter_request_new_pad (GstElement    *element,
  GstPadTemplate *templ,
```

```
                                     const gchar    *name,
                                     const GstCaps   *caps);

static void gst_my_filter_release_pad (GstElement *element,
                                       GstPad *pad);

static GstStaticPadTemplate sink_factory =
GST_STATIC_PAD_TEMPLATE (
  "sink_%u",
  GST_PAD_SINK,
  GST_PAD_REQUEST,
  GST_STATIC_CAPS ("ANY")
);

static void
gst_my_filter_class_init (GstMyFilterClass *klass)
{
  GstElementClass *element_class = GST_ELEMENT_CLASS (klass);
[..]
  gst_element_class_add_pad_template (klass,
gst_static_pad_template_get (&sink_factory));
[..]
  element_class->request_new_pad = gst_my_filter_request_new_pad;
  element_class->release_pad = gst_my_filter_release_pad;
}

static GstPad *
gst_my_filter_request_new_pad (GstElement     *element,
      GstPadTemplate *templ,
      const gchar    *name,
                                const GstCaps  *caps)
{
  GstPad *pad;
  GstMyFilterInputContext *context;

  context = g_new0 (GstMyFilterInputContext, 1);
  pad = gst_pad_new_from_template (templ, name);
  gst_pad_set_element_private (pad, context);

  /* normally, you would set _chain () and _event () functions here */

  gst_element_add_pad (element, pad);

  return pad;
}

static void
gst_my_filter_release_pad (GstElement *element,
                           GstPad *pad)
{
  GstMyFilterInputContext *context;

  context = gst_pad_get_element_private (pad);
```

```
  g_free (context);

  gst_element_remove_pad (element, pad);
}
```

Chapter 13. Different scheduling modes

The scheduling mode of a pad defines how data is retrieved from (source) or given to (sink) pads. GStreamer can operate in two scheduling mode, called push- and pull-mode. GStreamer supports elements with pads in any of the scheduling modes where not all pads need to be operating in the same mode.

So far, we have only discussed _chain ()-operating elements, i.e. elements that have a chain-function set on their sink pad and push buffers on their source pad(s). We call this the push-mode because a peer element will use gst_pad_push () on a srcpad, which will cause our _chain ()-function to be called, which in turn causes our element to push out a buffer on the source pad. The initiative to start the dataflow happens somewhere upstream when it pushes out a buffer and all downstream elements get scheduled when their _chain ()-functions are called in turn.

Before we explain pull-mode scheduling, let's first understand how the different scheduling modes are selected and activated on a pad.

13.1. The pad activation stage

During the element state change of READY->PAUSED, the pads of an element will be activated. This happens first on the source pads and then on the sink pads of the element. GStreamer calls the _activate () of a pad. By default this function will activate the pad in push-mode by calling gst_pad_activate_mode () with the GST_PAD_MODE_PUSH scheduling mode. It is possible to override the _activate () of a pad and decide on a different scheduling mode. You can know in what scheduling mode a pad is activated by overriding the _activate_mode ()-function.

GStreamer allows the different pads of an element to operate in different scheduling modes. This allows for many different possible use-cases. What follows is an overview of some typical use-cases.

- If all pads of an element are activated in push-mode scheduling, the element as a whole is operating in push-mode. For source elements this means that they will have to start a task that pushes out buffers on the source pad to the downstream elements. Downstream elements will have data pushed to them by upstream elements using the sinkpads _chain ()-function which will push out buffers on the source pads. Prerequisites for this scheduling mode are that a chain-function was set for each sinkpad using gst_pad_set_chain_function () and that all downstream elements operate in the same mode.

- Alternatively, sinkpads can be the driving force behind a pipeline by operating in pull-mode, while the sourcepads of the element still operate in push-mode. In order to be the driving force, those pads start a GstTask when they are activated. This task is a thread, which will call a function specified by the element. When called, this function will have random data access (through gst_pad_pull_range ()) over all sinkpads, and can push data over the sourcepads, which effectively means that this element controls data flow in the pipeline. Prerequisites for this mode are that all downstream elements can act in push mode, and that all upstream elements operate in pull-mode (see below).

Source pads can be activated in PULL mode by a downstream element when they return GST_PAD_MODE_PULL from the GST_QUERY_SCHEDULING query. Prerequisites for this scheduling mode are that a getrange-function was set for the source pad using `gst_pad_set_getrange_function ()`.

- Lastly, all pads in an element can be activated in PULL-mode. However, contrary to the above, this does not mean that they start a task on their own. Rather, it means that they are pull slave for the downstream element, and have to provide random data access to it from their `_get_range` `()`-function. Requirements are that the a `_get_range` `()`-function was set on this pad using the function `gst_pad_set_getrange_function ()`. Also, if the element has any sinkpads, all those pads (and thereby their peers) need to operate in PULL access mode, too.

When a sink element is activated in PULL mode, it should start a task that calls `gst_pad_pull_range ()` on its sinkpad. It can only do this when the upstream SCHEDULING query returns support for the GST_PAD_MODE_PULL scheduling mode.

In the next two sections, we will go closer into pull-mode scheduling (elements/pads driving the pipeline, and elements/pads providing random access), and some specific use cases will be given.

13.2. Pads driving the pipeline

Sinkpads operating in pull-mode, with the sourcepads operating in push-mode (or it has no sourcepads when it is a sink), can start a task that will drive the pipeline data flow. Within this task function, you have random access over all of the sinkpads, and push data over the sourcepads. This can come in useful for several different kinds of elements:

- Demuxers, parsers and certain kinds of decoders where data comes in unparsed (such as MPEG-audio or video streams), since those will prefer byte-exact (random) access from their input. If possible, however, such elements should be prepared to operate in push-mode mode, too.

- Certain kind of audio outputs, which require control over their input data flow, such as the Jack sound server.

First you need to perform a SCHEDULING query to check if the upstream element(s) support pull-mode scheduling. If that is possible, you can activate the sinkpad in pull-mode. Inside the activate_mode function you can then start the task.

```
#include "filter.h"
#include <string.h>

static gboolean gst_my_filter_activate      (GstPad       * pad,
                                             GstObject    * parent);
static gboolean gst_my_filter_activate_mode (GstPad       * pad,
                                             GstObject    * parent,
```

```
                                      GstPadMode    mode,
      gboolean      active);
static void gst_my_filter_loop      (GstMyFilter * filter);

G_DEFINE_TYPE (GstMyFilter, gst_my_filter, GST_TYPE_ELEMENT);


static void
gst_my_filter_init (GstMyFilter * filter)
{

[..]

  gst_pad_set_activate_function (filter->sinkpad, gst_my_filter_activate);
  gst_pad_set_activatemode_function (filter->sinkpad,
      gst_my_filter_activate_mode);


[..]
}

[..]

static gboolean
gst_my_filter_activate (GstPad * pad, GstObject * parent)
{
  GstQuery *query;
  gboolean pull_mode;

  /* first check what upstream scheduling is supported */
  query = gst_query_new_scheduling ();

  if (!gst_pad_peer_query (pad, query)) {
    gst_query_unref (query);
    goto activate_push;
  }

  /* see if pull-mode is supported */
  pull_mode = gst_query_has_scheduling_mode_with_flags (query,
      GST_PAD_MODE_PULL, GST_SCHEDULING_FLAG_SEEKABLE);
  gst_query_unref (query);

  if (!pull_mode)
    goto activate_push;

  /* now we can activate in pull-mode. GStreamer will also
   * activate the upstream peer in pull-mode */
  return gst_pad_activate_mode (pad, GST_PAD_MODE_PULL, TRUE);

activate_push:
  {
    /* something not right, we fallback to push-mode */
    return gst_pad_activate_mode (pad, GST_PAD_MODE_PUSH, TRUE);
```

```
    }
}

static gboolean
gst_my_filter_activate_pull (GstPad     * pad,
    GstObject * parent,
    GstPadMode   mode,
    gboolean     active)
{
  gboolean res;
  GstMyFilter *filter = GST_MY_FILTER (parent);

  switch (mode) {
    case GST_PAD_MODE_PUSH:
      res = TRUE;
      break;
    case GST_PAD_MODE_PULL:
      if (active) {
        filter->offset = 0;
        res = gst_pad_start_task (pad,
            (GstTaskFunction) gst_my_filter_loop, filter, NULL);
      } else {
        res = gst_pad_stop_task (pad);
      }
      break;
    default:
      /* unknown scheduling mode */
      res = FALSE;
      break;
  }
  return res;
}
```

Once started, your task has full control over input and output. The most simple case of a task function is one that reads input and pushes that over its source pad. It's not all that useful, but provides some more flexibility than the old push-mode case that we've been looking at so far.

```
#define BLOCKSIZE 2048

static void
gst_my_filter_loop (GstMyFilter * filter)
{
  GstFlowReturn ret;
  guint64 len;
  GstFormat fmt = GST_FORMAT_BYTES;
  GstBuffer *buf = NULL;

  if (!gst_pad_query_duration (filter->sinkpad, fmt, &len)) {
    GST_DEBUG_OBJECT (filter, "failed to query duration, pausing");
    goto stop;
  }
```

```
  if (filter->offset >= len) {
    GST_DEBUG_OBJECT (filter, "at end of input, sending EOS, pausing");
    gst_pad_push_event (filter->srcpad, gst_event_new_eos ());
    goto stop;
  }

  /* now, read BLOCKSIZE bytes from byte offset filter->offset */
  ret = gst_pad_pull_range (filter->sinkpad, filter->offset,
      BLOCKSIZE, &buf);

  if (ret != GST_FLOW_OK) {
    GST_DEBUG_OBJECT (filter, "pull_range failed: %s", gst_flow_get_name (ret));
    goto stop;
  }

  /* now push buffer downstream */
  ret = gst_pad_push (filter->srcpad, buf);

  buf = NULL; /* gst_pad_push() took ownership of buffer */

  if (ret != GST_FLOW_OK) {
    GST_DEBUG_OBJECT (filter, "pad_push failed: %s", gst_flow_get_name (ret));
    goto stop;
  }

  /* everything is fine, increase offset and wait for us to be called again */
  filter->offset += BLOCKSIZE;
  return;

stop:
  GST_DEBUG_OBJECT (filter, "pausing task");
  gst_pad_pause_task (filter->sinkpad);
}
```

13.3. Providing random access

In the previous section, we have talked about how elements (or pads) that are activated to drive the pipeline using their own task, must use pull-mode scheduling on their sinkpads. This means that all pads linked to those pads need to be activated in pull-mode. Source pads activated in pull-mode must implement a _get_range ()-function set using gst_pad_set_getrange_function (), and that function will be called when the peer pad requests some data with gst_pad_pull_range (). The element is then responsible for seeking to the right offset and providing the requested data. Several elements can implement random access:

- Data sources, such as a file source, that can provide data from any offset with reasonable low latency.

- Filters that would like to provide a pull-mode scheduling over the whole pipeline.

- Parsers who can easily provide this by skipping a small part of their input and are thus essentially "forwarding" getrange requests literally without any own processing involved. Examples include tag readers (e.g. ID3) or single output parsers, such as a WAVE parser.

The following example will show how a `_get_range ()`-function can be implemented in a source element:

```
#include "filter.h"
static GstFlowReturn
gst_my_filter_get_range (GstPad      * pad,
 GstObject  * parent,
 guint64      offset,
 guint        length,
 GstBuffer ** buf);

G_DEFINE_TYPE (GstMyFilter, gst_my_filter, GST_TYPE_ELEMENT);



static void
gst_my_filter_init (GstMyFilter * filter)
{

[..]

  gst_pad_set_getrange_function (filter->srcpad,
      gst_my_filter_get_range);

[..]
}

static GstFlowReturn
gst_my_filter_get_range (GstPad      * pad,
 GstObject  * parent,
 guint64      offset,
 guint        length,
 GstBuffer ** buf)
{

  GstMyFilter *filter = GST_MY_FILTER (parent);

  [.. here, you would fill *buf ..]

  return GST_FLOW_OK;
}
```

In practice, many elements that could theoretically do random access, may in practice often be activated in push-mode scheduling anyway, since there is no downstream element able to start its own task. Therefore, in practice, those elements should implement both a `_get_range ()`-function and a `_chain`

`()`-function (for filters and parsers) or a `_get_range` `()`-function and be prepared to start their own task by providing `_activate_*` `()`-functions (for source elements).

Chapter 14. Caps negotiation

Caps negotiation is the act of finding a media format (GstCaps) between elements that they can handle. This process in GStreamer can in most cases find an optimal solution for the complete pipeline. In this section we explain how this works.

14.1. Caps negotiation basics

In GStreamer, negotiation of the media format always follows the following simple rules:

- A downstream element suggest a format on its sinkpad and places the suggestion in the result of the CAPS query performed on the sinkpad. See also Implementing a CAPS query function.

- An upstream element decides on a format. It sends the selected media format downstream on its source pad with a CAPS event. Downstream elements reconfigure themselves to handle the media type in the CAPS event on the sinkpad.

- A downstream element can inform upstream that it would like to suggest a new format by sending a RECONFIGURE event upstream. The RECONFIGURE event simply instructs an upstream element to restart the negotiation phase. Because the element that sent out the RECONFIGURE event is now suggesting another format, the format in the pipeline might change.

In addition to the CAPS and RECONFIGURE event and the CAPS query, there is an ACCEPT_CAPS query to quickly check if a certain caps can be accepted by an element.

All negotiation follows these simple rules. Let's take a look at some typical uses cases and how negotiation happens.

14.2. Caps negotiation use cases

In what follows we will look at some use cases for push-mode scheduling. The pull-mode scheduling negotiation phase is discussed in Section 14.5 and is actually similar as we will see.

Since the sink pads only suggest formats and the source pads need to decide, the most complicated work is done in the source pads. We can identify 3 caps negotiation use cases for the source pads:

- Fixed negotiation. An element can output one format only. See Section 14.2.1.

- Transform negotiation. There is a (fixed) transform between the input and output format of the element, usually based on some element property. The caps that the element will produce depend on the upstream caps and the caps that the element can accept depend on the downstream caps. See Section 14.2.2.

- Dynamic negotiation. An element can output many formats. See Section 14.2.3.

14.2.1. Fixed negotiation

In this case, the source pad can only produce a fixed format. Usually this format is encoded inside the media. No downstream element can ask for a different format, the only way that the source pad will renegotiate is when the element decides to change the caps itself.

Elements that could implement fixed caps (on their source pads) are, in general, all elements that are not renegotiable. Examples include:

- A typefinder, since the type found is part of the actual data stream and can thus not be re-negotiated. The typefinder will look at the stream of bytes, figure out the type, send a CAPS event with the caps and then push buffers of the type.

- Pretty much all demuxers, since the contained elementary data streams are defined in the file headers, and thus not renegotiable.

- Some decoders, where the format is embedded in the data stream and not part of the peercaps *and* where the decoder itself is not reconfigurable, too.

- Some sources that produce a fixed format.

`gst_pad_use_fixed_caps()` is used on the source pad with fixed caps. As long as the pad is not negotiated, the default CAPS query will return the caps presented in the padtemplate. As soon as the pad is negotiated, the CAPS query will return the negotiated caps (and nothing else). These are the relevant code snippets for fixed caps source pads.

```
[..]
  pad = gst_pad_new_from_static_template (..);
  gst_pad_use_fixed_caps (pad);
[..]
```

The fixed caps can then be set on the pad by calling `gst_pad_set_caps ()`.

```
[..]
   caps = gst_caps_new_simple ("audio/x-raw",
       "format", G_TYPE_STRING, GST_AUDIO_NE(F32),
       "rate", G_TYPE_INT, <samplerate>,
       "channels", G_TYPE_INT, <num-channels>, NULL);
   if (!gst_pad_set_caps (pad, caps)) {
     GST_ELEMENT_ERROR (element, CORE, NEGOTIATION, (NULL),
         ("Some debug information here"));
     return GST_FLOW_ERROR;
   }
[..]
```

These types of elements also don't have a relation between the input format and the output format, the input caps simply don't contain the information needed to produce the output caps.

All other elements that need to be configured for the format should implement full caps negotiation, which will be explained in the next few sections.

14.2.2. Transform negotiation

In this negotiation technique, there is a fixed transform between the element input caps and the output caps. This transformation could be parameterized by element properties but not by the content of the stream (see Section 14.2.1 for that use-case).

The caps that the element can accept depend on the (fixed transformation) downstream caps. The caps that the element can produce depend on the (fixed transformation of) the upstream caps.

This type of element can usually set caps on its source pad from the _event() function on the sink pad when it received the CAPS event. This means that the caps transform function transforms a fixed caps into another fixed caps. Examples of elements include:

* Videobox. It adds configurable border around a video frame depending on object properties.

* Identity elements. All elements that don't change the format of the data, only the content. Video and audio effects are an example. Other examples include elements that inspect the stream.

* Some decoders and encoders, where the output format is defined by input format, like mulawdec and mulawenc. These decoders usually have no headers that define the content of the stream. They are usually more like conversion elements.

Below is an example of a negotiation steps of a typical transform element. In the sink pad CAPS event handler, we compute the caps for the source pad and set those.

```
  [...]

static gboolean
gst_my_filter_setcaps (GstMyFilter *filter,
      GstCaps *caps)
{
  GstStructure *structure;
  int rate, channels;
  gboolean ret;
  GstCaps *outcaps;

  structure = gst_caps_get_structure (caps, 0);
  ret = gst_structure_get_int (structure, "rate", &rate);
  ret = ret && gst_structure_get_int (structure, "channels", &channels);
  if (!ret)
```

```
    return FALSE;

  outcaps = gst_caps_new_simple ("audio/x-raw",
      "format", G_TYPE_STRING, GST_AUDIO_NE(S16),
      "rate", G_TYPE_INT, rate,
      "channels", G_TYPE_INT, channels, NULL);
  ret = gst_pad_set_caps (filter->srcpad, outcaps);
  gst_caps_unref (outcaps);

  return ret;
}

static gboolean
gst_my_filter_sink_event (GstPad    *pad,
        GstObject *parent,
        GstEvent  *event)
{
  gboolean ret;
  GstMyFilter *filter = GST_MY_FILTER (parent);

  switch (GST_EVENT_TYPE (event)) {
    case GST_EVENT_CAPS:
    {
      GstCaps *caps;

      gst_event_parse_caps (event, &caps);
      ret = gst_my_filter_setcaps (filter, caps);
      break;
    }
    default:
      ret = gst_pad_event_default (pad, parent, event);
      break;
  }
  return ret;
}

  [...]
```

14.2.3. Dynamic negotiation

A last negotiation method is the most complex and powerful dynamic negotiation.

Like with the transform negotiation in Section 14.2.2, dynamic negotiation will perform a transformation on the downstream/upstream caps. Unlike the transform negotiation, this transform will convert fixed caps to unfixed caps. This means that the sink pad input caps can be converted into unfixed (multiple) formats. The source pad will have to choose a format from all the possibilities. It would usually like to choose a format that requires the least amount of effort to produce but it does not have to be. The selection of the format should also depend on the caps that can be accepted downstream (see a QUERY_CAPS function in Implementing a CAPS query function).

A typical flow goes like this:

- Caps are received on the sink pad of the element.
- If the element prefers to operate in passthrough mode, check if downstream accepts the caps with the ACCEPT_CAPS query. If it does, we can complete negotiation and we can operate in passthrough mode.
- Calculate the possible caps for the source pad.
- Query the downstream peer pad for the list of possible caps.
- Select from the downstream list the first caps that you can transform to and set this as the output caps. You might have to fixate the caps to some reasonable defaults to construct fixed caps.

Examples of this type of elements include:

- Converter elements such as videoconvert, audioconvert, audioresample, videoscale, ...
- Source elements such as audiotestsrc, videotestsrc, v4l2src, pulsesrc, ...

Let's look at the example of an element that can convert between samplerates, so where input and output samplerate don't have to be the same:

```
static gboolean
gst_my_filter_setcaps (GstMyFilter *filter,
      GstCaps *caps)
{
  if (gst_pad_set_caps (filter->srcpad, caps)) {
    filter->passthrough = TRUE;
  } else {
    GstCaps *othercaps, *newcaps;
    GstStructure *s = gst_caps_get_structure (caps, 0), *others;

    /* no passthrough, setup internal conversion */
    gst_structure_get_int (s, "channels", &filter->channels);
    othercaps = gst_pad_get_allowed_caps (filter->srcpad);
    others = gst_caps_get_structure (othercaps, 0);
    gst_structure_set (others,
      "channels", G_TYPE_INT, filter->channels, NULL);

    /* now, the samplerate value can optionally have multiple values, so
     * we "fixate" it, which means that one fixed value is chosen */
    newcaps = gst_caps_copy_nth (othercaps, 0);
    gst_caps_unref (othercaps);
    gst_pad_fixate_caps (filter->srcpad, newcaps);
    if (!gst_pad_set_caps (filter->srcpad, newcaps))
      return FALSE;
```

```
      /* we are now set up, configure internally */
      filter->passthrough = FALSE;
      gst_structure_get_int (s, "rate", &filter->from_samplerate);
      others = gst_caps_get_structure (newcaps, 0);
      gst_structure_get_int (others, "rate", &filter->to_samplerate);
  }

  return TRUE;
}

static gboolean
gst_my_filter_sink_event (GstPad    *pad,
          GstObject *parent,
          GstEvent  *event)
{
  gboolean ret;
  GstMyFilter *filter = GST_MY_FILTER (parent);

  switch (GST_EVENT_TYPE (event)) {
    case GST_EVENT_CAPS:
    {
      GstCaps *caps;

      gst_event_parse_caps (event, &caps);
      ret = gst_my_filter_setcaps (filter, caps);
      break;
    }
    default:
      ret = gst_pad_event_default (pad, parent, event);
      break;
  }
  return ret;
}

static GstFlowReturn
gst_my_filter_chain (GstPad    *pad,
    GstObject *parent,
    GstBuffer *buf)
{
  GstMyFilter *filter = GST_MY_FILTER (parent);
  GstBuffer *out;

  /* push on if in passthrough mode */
  if (filter->passthrough)
    return gst_pad_push (filter->srcpad, buf);

  /* convert, push */
  out = gst_my_filter_convert (filter, buf);
  gst_buffer_unref (buf);

  return gst_pad_push (filter->srcpad, out);
}
```

14.3. Upstream caps (re)negotiation

Upstream negotiation's primary use is to renegotiate (part of) an already-negotiated pipeline to a new format. Some practical examples include to select a different video size because the size of the video window changed, and the video output itself is not capable of rescaling, or because the audio channel configuration changed.

Upstream caps renegotiation is requested by sending a GST_EVENT_RECONFIGURE event upstream. The idea is that it will instruct the upstream element to reconfigure its caps by doing a new query for the allowed caps and then choosing a new caps. The element that sends out the RECONFIGURE event would influence the selection of the new caps by returning the new preferred caps from its GST_QUERY_CAPS query function. The RECONFIGURE event will set the GST_PAD_FLAG_NEED_RECONFIGURE on all pads that it travels over.

It is important to note here that different elements actually have different responsibilities here:

- Elements that want to propose a new format upstream need to first check if the new caps are acceptable upstream with an ACCEPT_CAPS query. Then they would send a RECONFIGURE event and be prepared to answer the CAPS query with the new preferred format. It should be noted that when there is no upstream element that can (or wants) to renegotiate, the element needs to deal with the currently configured format.

- Elements that operate in transform negotiation according to Section 14.2.2 pass the RECONFIGURE event upstream. Because these elements simply do a fixed transform based on the upstream caps, they need to send the event upstream so that it can select a new format.

- Elements that operate in fixed negotiation (Section 14.2.1) drop the RECONFIGURE event. These elements can't reconfigure and their output caps don't depend on the upstream caps so the event can be dropped.

- Elements that can be reconfigured on the source pad (source pads implementing dynamic negotiation in Section 14.2.3) should check its NEED_RECONFIGURE flag with `gst_pad_check_reconfigure ()` and it should start renegotiation when the function returns TRUE.

14.4. Implementing a CAPS query function

A `_query ()`-function with the GST_QUERY_CAPS query type is called when a peer element would like to know which formats this pad supports, and in what order of preference. The return value should be all formats that this elements supports, taking into account limitations of peer elements further downstream or upstream, sorted by order of preference, highest preference first.

```
static gboolean
gst_my_filter_query (GstPad *pad, GstObject * parent, GstQuery * query)
{
  gboolean ret;
  GstMyFilter *filter = GST_MY_FILTER (parent);

  switch (GST_QUERY_TYPE (query)) {
    case GST_QUERY_CAPS
    {
      GstPad *otherpad;
      GstCaps *temp, *caps, *filt, *tcaps;
      gint i;

      otherpad = (pad == filter->srcpad) ? filter->sinkpad :
                                           filter->srcpad;
      caps = gst_pad_get_allowed_caps (otherpad);

      gst_query_parse_caps (query, &filt);

      /* We support *any* samplerate, indifferent from the samplerate
       * supported by the linked elements on both sides. */
      for (i = 0; i < gst_caps_get_size (caps); i++) {
        GstStructure *structure = gst_caps_get_structure (caps, i);

        gst_structure_remove_field (structure, "rate");
      }

      /* make sure we only return results that intersect our
       * padtemplate */
      tcaps = gst_pad_get_pad_template_caps (pad);
      if (tcaps) {
        temp = gst_caps_intersect (caps, tcaps);
        gst_caps_unref (caps);
        gst_caps_unref (tcaps);
        caps = temp;
      }
      /* filter against the query filter when needed */
      if (filt) {
        temp = gst_caps_intersect (caps, filt);
        gst_caps_unref (caps);
        caps = temp;
      }
      gst_query_set_caps_result (query, caps);
      gst_caps_unref (caps);
      ret = TRUE;
      break;
    }
    default:
      ret = gst_pad_query_default (pad, parent, query);
      break;
  }
  return ret;
```

}

14.5. Pull-mode Caps negotiation

WRITEME, the mechanism of pull-mode negotiation is not yet fully understood.

Using all the knowledge you've acquired by reading this chapter, you should be able to write an element that does correct caps negotiation. If in doubt, look at other elements of the same type in our git repository to get an idea of how they do what you want to do.

Chapter 15. Memory allocation

Memory allocation and management is a very important topic in multimedia. High definition video uses many megabytes to store one single frame of video. It is important to reuse the memory when possible instead of constantly allocating and freeing the memory.

Multimedia systems usually use special purpose chips, such as DSPs or GPUs to perform the heavy lifting (especially for video). These special purpose chips have usually strict requirements for the memory that they can operate on and how the memory is accessed.

This chapter talks about the memory management features that GStreamer plugins can use. We will first talk about the lowlevel `GstMemory` object that manages access to a piece of memory. We then continue with `GstBuffer` that is used to exchange data between plugins (and the application) and that uses `GstMemory`. We talk about `GstMeta` that can be placed on buffers to give extra info about the buffer and its memory. For efficiently managing buffers of the same size, we take a look at `GstBufferPool`. To conclude this chapter we take a look at the GST_QUERY_ALLOCATION query that is used to negotiate memory management options between elements.

15.1. GstMemory

`GstMemory` is an object that manages a region of memory. The memory object points to a region of memory of "maxsize". The area in this memory starting at "offset" and for "size" bytes is the accessible region in the memory. the maxsize of the memory can never be changed after the object is created, however, the offset and size can be changed.

15.1.1. GstAllocator

`GstMemory` objects are created by a `GstAllocator` object. Most allocators implement the default `gst_allocator_alloc()` method but some allocator might implement a different method, for example when additional parameters are needed to allocate the specific memory.

Different allocators exist for, for example, system memory, shared memory and memory backed by a DMAbuf file descriptor. To implement support for a new kind of memory type, you must implement a new allocator object as shown below.

15.1.2. GstMemory API example

Data access to the memory wrapped by the `GstMemory` object is always protected with a `gst_memory_map()` and `gst_memory_unmap()` pair. An access mode (read/write) must be given when mapping memory. The map function returns a pointer to the valid memory region that can then be accessed according to the requested access mode.

Below is an example of making a `GstMemory` object and using the `gst_memory_map()` to access the memory region.

```
[...]

  GstMemory *mem;
  GstMapInfo info;
  gint i;

  /* allocate 100 bytes */
  mem = gst_allocator_alloc (NULL, 100, NULL);

  /* get access to the memory in write mode */
  gst_memory_map (mem, &info, GST_MAP_WRITE);

  /* fill with pattern */
  for (i = 0; i < info.size; i++)
    info.data[i] = i;

  /* release memory */
  gst_memory_unmap (mem, &info);

[...]
```

15.1.3. Implementing a GstAllocator

WRITEME

15.2. GstBuffer

A `GstBuffer` is an lightweight object that is passed from an upstream to a downstream element and contains memory and metadata. It represents the multimedia content that is pushed or pull downstream by elements.

The buffer contains one or more `GstMemory` objects that represent the data in the buffer.

Metadata in the buffer consists of:

- DTS and PTS timestamps. These represent the decoding and presentation timestamps of the buffer content and is used by synchronizing elements to schedule buffers. Both these timestamps can be GST_CLOCK_TIME_NONE when unknown/undefined.

- The duration of the buffer contents. This duration can be GST_CLOCK_TIME_NONE when unknown/undefined.

- Media specific offsets and offset_end. For video this is the frame number in the stream and for audio the sample number. Other definitions for other media exist.

- Arbitrary structures via GstMeta, see below.

15.2.1. GstBuffer writability

A buffer is writable when the refcount of the object is exactly 1, meaning that only one object is holding a ref to the buffer. You can only modify anything in the buffer when the buffer is writable. This means that you need to call gst_buffer_make_writable() before changing the timestamps, offsets, metadata or adding and removing memory blocks.

15.2.2. GstBuffer API examples

You can create a buffer with gst_buffer_new () and then add memory objects to it or you can use a convenience function gst_buffer_new_allocate () which combines the two. It's also possible to wrap existing memory with gst_buffer_new_wrapped_full () where you can give the function to call when the memory should be freed.

You can access the memory of the buffer by getting and mapping the GstMemory objects individually or by using gst_buffer_map (). The latter merges all the memory into one big block and then gives you a pointer to this block.

Below is an example of how to create a buffer and access its memory.

```
[...]
  GstBuffer *buffer;
  GstMemory *mem;
  GstMapInfo info;

  /* make empty buffer */
  buffer = gst_buffer_new ();

  /* make memory holding 100 bytes */
  mem = gst_allocator_alloc (NULL, 100, NULL);

  /* add the buffer */
  gst_buffer_append_memory (buffer, mem);
```

```
[...]

  /* get WRITE access to the memory and fill with 0xff */
  gst_buffer_map (buffer, &info, GST_MAP_WRITE);
  memset (info.data, 0xff, info.size);
  gst_buffer_unmap (buffer, &info);

[...]

  /* free the buffer */
  gst_buffer_unref (buffer);

[...]
```

15.3. GstMeta

With the `GstMeta` system you can add arbitrary structures on buffers. These structures describe extra properties of the buffer such as cropping, stride, region of interest etc.

The metadata system separates API specification (what the metadata and its API look like) and the implementation (how it works). This makes it possible to make different implementations of the same API, for example, depending on the hardware you are running on.

15.3.1. GstMeta API example

After allocating a new buffer, you can add metadata to the buffer with the metadata specific API. This means that you will need to link to the header file where the metadata is defined to use its API.

By convention, a metadata API with name `FooBar` should provide two methods, a `gst_buffer_add_foo_bar_meta ()` and a `gst_buffer_get_foo_bar_meta ()`. Both functions should return a pointer to a `FooBarMeta` structure that contains the metadata fields. Some of the `_add_*_meta ()` can have extra parameters that will usually be used to configure the metadata structure for you.

Let's have a look at the metadata that is used to specify a cropping region for video frames.

```
#include <gst/video/gstvideometa.h>

[...]
  GstVideoCropMeta *meta;
```

```
  /* buffer points to a video frame, add some cropping metadata */
  meta = gst_buffer_add_video_crop_meta (buffer);

  /* configure the cropping metadata */
  meta->x = 8;
  meta->y = 8;
  meta->width = 120;
  meta->height = 80;
[...]
```

An element can then use the metadata on the buffer when rendering the frame like this:

```
#include <gst/video/gstvideometa.h>

[...]
  GstVideoCropMeta *meta;

  /* buffer points to a video frame, get the cropping metadata */
  meta = gst_buffer_get_video_crop_meta (buffer);

  if (meta) {
    /* render frame with cropping */
    _render_frame_cropped (buffer, meta->x, meta->y, meta->width, meta->height);
  } else {
    /* render frame */
    _render_frame (buffer);
  }
[...]
```

15.3.2. Implementing new GstMeta

In the next sections we show how you can add new metadata to the system and use it on buffers.

15.3.2.1. Define the metadata API

First we need to define what our API will look like and we will have to register this API to the system. This is important because this API definition will be used when elements negotiate what kind of metadata they will exchange. The API definition also contains arbitrary tags that give hints about what the metadata contains. This is important when we see how metadata is preserved when buffers pass through the pipeline.

If you are making a new implementation of an existing API, you can skip this step and move on to the implementation step.

First we start with making the `my-example-meta.h` header file that will contain the definition of the API and structure for our metadata.

```
#include <gst/gst.h>

typedef struct _MyExampleMeta MyExampleMeta;

struct _MyExampleMeta {
  GstMeta         meta;

  gint            age;
  gchar          *name;
};

GType my_example_meta_api_get_type (void);
#define MY_EXAMPLE_META_API_TYPE (my_example_meta_api_get_type())

#define gst_buffer_get_my_example_meta(b) \
  ((MyExampleMeta*)gst_buffer_get_meta((b),MY_EXAMPLE_META_API_TYPE))
```

The metadata API definition consists of the definition of the structure that holds a gint and a string. The first field in the structure must be `GstMeta`.

We also define a `my_example_meta_api_get_type` () function that will register out metadata API definition. We also define a convenience macro `gst_buffer_get_my_example_meta` () that simply finds and returns the metadata with our new API.

Next let's have a look at how the `my_example_meta_api_get_type` () function is implemented in the `my-example-meta.c` file.

```
#include "my-example-meta.h"

GType
my_example_meta_api_get_type (void)
{
  static volatile GType type;
  static const gchar *tags[] = { "foo", "bar", NULL };

  if (g_once_init_enter (&type)) {
    GType _type = gst_meta_api_type_register ("MyExampleMetaAPI", tags);
    g_once_init_leave (&type, _type);
  }
```

```
    return type;
}
```

As you can see, it simply uses the `gst_meta_api_type_register ()` function to register a name for the api and some tags. The result is a new pointer GType that defines the newly registered API.

15.3.2.2. Implementing a metadata API

Next we can make an implementation for a registered metadata API GType. The implementation detail of a metadata API are kept in a `GstMetaInfo` structure that you will make available to the users of your metadata API implementation with a `my_example_meta_get_info ()` function and a convenience `MY_EXAMPLE_META_INFO` macro. You will also make a method to add your metadata implementation to a `GstBuffer`. Your `my-example-meta.h` header file will need these additions:

```
[...]

/* implementation */
const GstMetaInfo *my_example_meta_get_info (void);
#define MY_EXAMPLE_META_INFO (my_example_meta_get_info())

MyExampleMeta * gst_buffer_add_my_example_meta (GstBuffer     *buffer,
                                                gint           age,
                                                const gchar   *name);
```

Let's have a look at how these functions are implemented in the `my-example-meta.c` file.

```
[...]

static gboolean
my_example_meta_init (GstMeta * meta, gpointer params, GstBuffer * buffer)
{
  MyExampleMeta *emeta = (MyExampleMeta *) meta;

  emeta->age = 0;
  emeta->name = NULL;

  return TRUE;
}

static gboolean
my_example_meta_transform (GstBuffer * transbuf, GstMeta * meta,
    GstBuffer * buffer, GQuark type, gpointer data)
{
```

```
  MyExampleMeta *emeta = (MyExampleMeta *) meta;

  /* we always copy no matter what transform */
  gst_buffer_add_my_example_meta (transbuf, emeta->age, emeta->name);

  return TRUE;
}

static void
my_example_meta_free (GstMeta * meta, GstBuffer * buffer)
{
  MyExampleMeta *emeta = (MyExampleMeta *) meta;

  g_free (emeta->name);
  emeta->name = NULL;
}

const GstMetaInfo *
my_example_meta_get_info (void)
{
  static const GstMetaInfo *meta_info = NULL;

  if (g_once_init_enter (&meta_info)) {
    const GstMetaInfo *mi = gst_meta_register (MY_EXAMPLE_META_API_TYPE,
        "MyExampleMeta",
        sizeof (MyExampleMeta),
        my_example_meta_init,
        my_example_meta_free,
        my_example_meta_transform);
    g_once_init_leave (&meta_info, mi);
  }
  return meta_info;
}

MyExampleMeta *
gst_buffer_add_my_example_meta (GstBuffer    *buffer,
                                gint          age,
                                const gchar *name)
{
  MyExampleMeta *meta;

  g_return_val_if_fail (GST_IS_BUFFER (buffer), NULL);

  meta = (MyExampleMeta *) gst_buffer_add_meta (buffer,
      MY_EXAMPLE_META_INFO, NULL);

  meta->age = age;
  meta->name = g_strdup (name);

  return meta;
}
```

`gst_meta_register ()` registers the implementation details, like the API that you implement and the size of the metadata structure along with methods to initialize and free the memory area. You can also implement a transform function that will be called when a certain transformation (identified by the quark and quark specific data) is performed on a buffer.

Lastly, you implement a `gst_buffer_add_*_meta()` that adds the metadata implementation to a buffer and sets the values of the metadata.

15.4. GstBufferPool

The `GstBufferPool` object provides a convenient base class for managing lists of reusable buffers. Essential for this object is that all the buffers have the same properties such as size, padding, metadata and alignment.

A bufferpool object can be configured to manage a minimum and maximum amount of buffers of a specific size. A bufferpool can also be configured to use a specific `GstAllocator` for the memory of the buffers. There is support in the bufferpool to enable bufferpool specific options, such as adding `GstMeta` to the buffers in the pool or such as enabling specific padding on the memory in the buffers.

A Bufferpool can be inactivate and active. In the inactive state, you can configure the pool. In the active state, you can't change the configuration anymore but you can acquire and release buffers from/to the pool.

In the following sections we take a look at how you can use a bufferpool.

15.4.1. GstBufferPool API example

Many different bufferpool implementations can exist; they are all subclasses of the base class `GstBufferPool`. For this example, we will assume we somehow have access to a bufferpool, either because we created it ourselves or because we were given one as a result of the ALLOCATION query as we will see below.

The bufferpool is initially in the inactive state so that we can configure it. Trying to configure a bufferpool that is not in the inactive state will fail. Likewise, trying to activate a bufferpool that is not configured will fail.

```
  GstStructure *config;

[...]
```

```
/* get config structure */
config = gst_buffer_pool_get_config (pool);

/* set caps, size, minimum and maximum buffers in the pool */
gst_buffer_pool_config_set_params (config, caps, size, min, max);

/* configure allocator and parameters */
gst_buffer_pool_config_set_allocator (config, allocator, &params);

/* store the updated configuration again */
gst_buffer_pool_set_config (pool, config);

[...]
```

The configuration of the bufferpool is maintained in a generic `GstStructure` that can be obtained with `gst_buffer_pool_get_config()`. Convenience methods exist to get and set the configuration options in this structure. After updating the structure, it is set as the current configuration in the bufferpool again with `gst_buffer_pool_set_config()`.

The following options can be configured on a bufferpool:

- The caps of the buffers to allocate.
- The size of the buffers. This is the suggested size of the buffers in the pool. The pool might decide to allocate larger buffers to add padding.
- The minimum and maximum amount of buffers in the pool. When minimum is set to > 0, the bufferpool will pre-allocate this amount of buffers. When maximum is not 0, the bufferpool will allocate up to maximum amount of buffers.
- The allocator and parameters to use. Some bufferpools might ignore the allocator and use its internal one.
- Other arbitrary bufferpool options identified with a string. a bufferpool lists the supported options with `gst_buffer_pool_get_options()` and you can ask if an option is supported with `gst_buffer_pool_has_option()`. The option can be enabled by adding it to the configuration structure with `gst_buffer_pool_config_add_option ()`. These options are used to enable things like letting the pool set metadata on the buffers or to add extra configuration options for padding, for example.

After the configuration is set on the bufferpool, the pool can be activated with `gst_buffer_pool_set_active (pool, TRUE)`. From that point on you can use `gst_buffer_pool_acquire_buffer ()` to retrieve a buffer from the pool, like this:

```
[...]

GstFlowReturn ret;
GstBuffer *buffer;
```

```
ret = gst_buffer_pool_acquire_buffer (pool, &buffer, NULL);
if (G_UNLIKELY (ret != GST_FLOW_OK))
  goto pool_failed;

[...]
```

It is important to check the return value of the acquire function because it is possible that it fails: When your element shuts down, it will deactivate the bufferpool and then all calls to acquire will return GST_FLOW_FLUSHNG.

All buffers that are acquired from the pool will have their pool member set to the original pool. When the last ref is decremented on the buffer, GStreamer will automatically call `gst_buffer_pool_release_buffer ()` to release the buffer back to the pool. You (or any other downstream element) don't need to know if a buffer came from a pool, you can just unref it.

15.4.2. Implementing a new GstBufferPool

WRITEME

15.5. GST_QUERY_ALLOCATION

The ALLOCATION query is used to negotiate `GstMeta`, `GstBufferPool` and `GstAllocator` between elements. Negotiation of the allocation strategy is always initiated and decided by a srcpad after it has negotiated a format and before it decides to push buffers. A sinkpad can suggest an allocation strategy but it is ultimately the source pad that will decide based on the suggestions of the downstream sink pad.

The source pad will do a GST_QUERY_ALLOCATION with the negotiated caps as a parameter. This is needed so that the downstream element knows what media type is being handled. A downstream sink pad can answer the allocation query with the following results:

- An array of possible `GstBufferPool` suggestions with suggested size, minimum and maximum amount of buffers.

- An array of GstAllocator objects along with suggested allocation parameters such as flags, prefix, alignment and padding. These allocators can also be configured in a bufferpool when this is supported by the bufferpool.

- An array of supported `GstMeta` implementations along with metadata specific parameters. It is important that the upstream element knows what kind of metadata is supported downstream before it places that metadata on buffers.

When the GST_QUERY_ALLOCATION returns, the source pad will select from the available bufferpools, allocators and metadata how it will allocate buffers.

15.5.1. ALLOCATION query example

Below is an example of the ALLOCATION query.

```
#include <gst/video/video.h>
#include <gst/video/gstvideometa.h>
#include <gst/video/gstvideopool.h>

  GstCaps *caps;
  GstQuery *query;
  GstStructure *structure;
  GstBufferPool *pool;
  GstStructure *config;
  guint size, min, max;

[...]

  /* find a pool for the negotiated caps now */
  query = gst_query_new_allocation (caps, TRUE);

  if (!gst_pad_peer_query (scope->srcpad, query)) {
    /* query failed, not a problem, we use the query defaults */
  }

  if (gst_query_get_n_allocation_pools (query) > 0) {
    /* we got configuration from our peer, parse them */
    gst_query_parse_nth_allocation_pool (query, 0, &pool, &size, &min, &max);
  } else {
    pool = NULL;
    size = 0;
    min = max = 0;
  }

  if (pool == NULL) {
    /* we did not get a pool, make one ourselves then */
    pool = gst_video_buffer_pool_new ();
  }

  config = gst_buffer_pool_get_config (pool);
  gst_buffer_pool_config_add_option (config, GST_BUFFER_POOL_OPTION_VIDEO_META);
  gst_buffer_pool_config_set_params (config, caps, size, min, max);
  gst_buffer_pool_set_config (pool, config);

  /* and activate */
  gst_buffer_pool_set_active (pool, TRUE);

[...]
```

This particular implementation will make a custom `GstVideoBufferPool` object that is specialized in allocating video buffers. You can also enable the pool to put `GstVideoMeta` metadata on the buffers from the pool doing `gst_buffer_pool_config_add_option (config,` `GST_BUFFER_POOL_OPTION_VIDEO_META)`.

15.5.2. The ALLOCATION query in base classes

In many baseclasses you will see the following virtual methods for influencing the allocation strategy:

- `propose_allocation ()` should suggest allocation parameters for the upstream element.
- `decide_allocation ()` should decide the allocation parameters from the suggestions received from downstream.

Implementors of these methods should modify the given `GstQuery` object by updating the pool options and allocation options.

Chapter 16. Types and Properties

There is a very large set of possible types that may be used to pass data between elements. Indeed, each new element that is defined may use a new data format (though unless at least one other element recognises that format, it will be most likely be useless since nothing will be able to link with it).

In order for types to be useful, and for systems like autopluggers to work, it is necessary that all elements agree on the type definitions, and which properties are required for each type. The GStreamer framework itself simply provides the ability to define types and parameters, but does not fix the meaning of types and parameters, and does not enforce standards on the creation of new types. This is a matter for a policy to decide, not technical systems to enforce.

For now, the policy is simple:

- Do not create a new type if you could use one which already exists.
- If creating a new type, discuss it first with the other GStreamer developers, on at least one of: IRC, mailing lists.
- Try to ensure that the name for a new format is as unlikely to conflict with anything else created already, and is not a more generalised name than it should be. For example: "audio/compressed" would be too generalised a name to represent audio data compressed with an mp3 codec. Instead "audio/mp3" might be an appropriate name, or "audio/compressed" could exist and have a property indicating the type of compression used.
- Ensure that, when you do create a new type, you specify it clearly, and get it added to the list of known types so that other developers can use the type correctly when writing their elements.

16.1. Building a Simple Format for Testing

If you need a new format that has not yet been defined in our List of Defined Types, you will want to have some general guidelines on media type naming, properties and such. A media type would ideally be equivalent to the Mime-type defined by IANA; else, it should be in the form type/x-name, where type is the sort of data this media type handles (audio, video, ...) and name should be something specific for this specific type. Audio and video media types should try to support the general audio/video properties (see the list), and can use their own properties, too. To get an idea of what properties we think are useful, see (again) the list.

Take your time to find the right set of properties for your type. There is no reason to hurry. Also, experimenting with this is generally a good idea. Experience learns that theoretically thought-out types are good, but they still need practical use to assure that they serve their needs. Make sure that your property names do not clash with similar properties used in other types. If they match, make sure they mean the same thing; properties with different types but the same names are *not* allowed.

16.2. Typefind Functions and Autoplugging

With only *defining* the types, we're not yet there. In order for a random data file to be recognized and played back as such, we need a way of recognizing their type out of the blue. For this purpose, "typefinding" was introduced. Typefinding is the process of detecting the type of a data stream. Typefinding consists of two separate parts: first, there's an unlimited number of functions that we call *typefind functions*, which are each able to recognize one or more types from an input stream. Then, secondly, there's a small engine which registers and calls each of those functions. This is the typefind core. On top of this typefind core, you would normally write an autoplugger, which is able to use this type detection system to dynamically build a pipeline around an input stream. Here, we will focus only on typefind functions.

A typefind function usually lives in `gst-plugins-base/gst/typefind/gsttypefindfunctions.c`, unless there's a good reason (like library dependencies) to put it elsewhere. The reason for this centralization is to reduce the number of plugins that need to be loaded in order to detect a stream's type. Below is an example that will recognize AVI files, which start with a "RIFF" tag, then the size of the file and then an "AVI " tag:

```
static void
gst_my_typefind_function (GstTypeFind *tf,
  gpointer      data)
{
  guint8 *data = gst_type_find_peek (tf, 0, 12);

  if (data &&
      GUINT32_FROM_LE (&((guint32 *) data)[0]) == GST_MAKE_FOURCC ('R','I','F','F') &&
      GUINT32_FROM_LE (&((guint32 *) data)[2]) == GST_MAKE_FOURCC ('A','V','I',' ')) {
    gst_type_find_suggest (tf, GST_TYPE_FIND_MAXIMUM,
    gst_caps_new_simple ("video/x-msvideo", NULL));
  }
}

static gboolean
plugin_init (GstPlugin *plugin)
{
  if (!gst_type_find_register (plugin, "", GST_RANK_PRIMARY,
      gst_my_typefind_function, "avi",
      gst_caps_new_simple ("video/x-msvideo",
    NULL), NULL))
    return FALSE;
}
```

Note that `gst-plugins/gst/typefind/gsttypefindfunctions.c` has some simplification macros to decrease the amount of code. Make good use of those if you want to submit typefinding patches with new typefind functions.

Autoplugging has been discussed in great detail in the Application Development Manual.

16.3. List of Defined Types

Below is a list of all the defined types in GStreamer. They are split up in separate tables for audio, video, container, subtitle and other types, for the sake of readability. Below each table might follow a list of notes that apply to that table. In the definition of each type, we try to follow the types and rules as defined by IANA (http://www.iana.org/assignments/media-types) for as far as possible.

Jump directly to a specific table:

- Table of Audio Types
- Table of Video Types
- Table of Container Types
- Table of Subtitle Types
- Table of Other Types

Note that many of the properties are not *required*, but rather *optional* properties. This means that most of these properties can be extracted from the container header, but that - in case the container header does not provide these - they can also be extracted by parsing the stream header or the stream content. The policy is that your element should provide the data that it knows about by only parsing its own content, not another element's content. Example: the AVI header provides samplerate of the contained audio stream in the header. MPEG system streams don't. This means that an AVI stream demuxer would provide samplerate as a property for MPEG audio streams, whereas an MPEG demuxer would not. A decoder needing this data would require a stream parser in between two extract this from the header or calculate it from the stream.

Table 16-1. Table of Audio Types

Media Type	Description	Property	Property Type	Property Values	Property Description
All audio types.					
audio/*	*All audio types*	rate	integer	greater than 0	The sample rate of the data, in samples (per channel) per second.
		channels	integer	greater than 0	The number of channels of audio data.

Media Type	Description	Property	Property Type	Property Values	Property Description
channel-mask	bitmask		Channel positions present. See "GstAudioChannelPosition". 0 means unpositioned.		
format	string	S8 U8 S16LE S16BE U16LE U16BE S24_32LE S24_32BE U24_32LE U24_32BE S32LE S32BE U32LE U32BE S24LE S24BE U24LE U24BE S20LE S20BE U20LE U20BE S18LE S18BE U18LE U18BE F32LE F32BE F64LE F64BE	The format of the sample data.	

Media Type	Description	Property	Property Type	Property Values	Property Description
layout	string		"interleaved" or "non-interleaved"		Layout of channels within a buffer.
All raw audio types.					
audio/x-raw	Unstructured and uncompressed raw audio data.				All properties (except channel-mask, in the mono and stereo cases) are mandatory.
All encoded audio types.					
audio/x-ac3	AC-3 or A52 audio streams.				There are currently no specific properties defined or needed for this type.
audio/x-adpcm	ADPCM Audio streams.	layout	string	"quick-time", "dvi", "mi-crosoft" or "4xm".	The layout defines the packing of the samples in the stream. In ADPCM, most formats store multiple samples per channel together. This number of samples differs per format, hence the different layouts. On the long term, we probably want this variable to die and use something more descriptive, but this will do for now.
	block_align	integer	Any	Chunk buffer size.	
audio/x-cinepak	Audio as provided in a Cinepak (Quicktime) stream.				There are currently no specific properties defined or needed for this type.
audio/x-dv	Audio as provided in a Digital Video stream.				There are currently no specific properties defined or needed for this type.

Media Type	Description	Property Name	Property Type	Property Values	Property Description
audio/x-flac	Free Lossless Audio codec (FLAC).				There are currently no specific properties defined or needed for this type.
audio/x-gsm	Data encoded by the GSM codec.				There are currently no specific properties defined or needed for this type.
audio/x-alaw	A-Law Audio.				There are currently no specific properties defined or needed for this type.
audio/x-mulaw	Mu-Law Audio.				There are currently no specific properties defined or needed for this type.
audio/x-mace	MACE Audio (used in Quick-time).	maceversion	integer	3 or 6	The version of the MACE audio codec used to encode the stream.
audio/mpeg	Audio data compressed using the MPEG audio encoding scheme.	mpegversion	integer	1, 2 or 4	The MPEG-version used for encoding the data. The value 1 refers to MPEG-1, -2 and -2.5 layer 1, 2 or 3. The values 2 and 4 refer to the MPEG-AAC audio encoding schemes.

Media Type	Description	Property	Property Type	Property Values	Property Description
framed	boolean	0 or 1			A true value indicates that each buffer contains exactly one frame. A false value indicates that frames and buffers do not necessarily match up.
layer	integer	1, 2, or 3			The compression scheme layer used to compress the data *(only if mpegversion=1)*.
bitrate	integer	greater than 0			The bitrate, in bits per second. For VBR (variable bitrate) MPEG data, this is the average bitrate.

Media Type	Description	Property Name	Property Type	Property Values	Property Description
audio/x-qdm2	Data encoded by the QDM version 2 codec.				There are currently no specific properties defined or needed for this type.
audio/x-pn-realaudio	Realmedia Audio data.	raversion	integer	1 or 2	The version of the Real Audio codec used to encode the stream. 1 stands for a 14k4 stream, 2 stands for a 28k8 stream.
audio/x-speex	Data encoded by the Speex audio codec				There are currently no specific properties defined or needed for this type.
audio/x-vorbis	Vorbis audio data				There are currently no specific properties defined or needed for this type.
audio/x-wma	Windows Media Audio	wmaversion	integer	1,2 or 3	The version of the WMA codec used to encode the stream.
audio/x-paris	Ensoniq PARIS audio				There are currently no specific properties defined or needed for this type.
audio/x-svx	Amiga IFF / SVX8 / SV16 audio				There are currently no specific properties defined or needed for this type.
audio/x-nist	Sphere NIST audio				There are currently no specific properties defined or needed for this type.
audio/x-voc	Sound Blaster VOC audio				There are currently no specific properties defined or needed for this type.
audio/x-ircam	Berkeley/IRCAM/CARL audio				There are currently no specific properties defined or needed for this type.

Media Type	Description	Property	Property Type	Property Values	Property Description
audio/x-w64	Sonic Foundry's 64 bit RIFF/WAV				There are currently no specific properties defined or needed for this type.

Table 16-2. Table of Video Types

Media Type	Description	Property	Property Type	Property Values	Property Description
All video types.					
video/*	*All video types*	width	integer	greater than 0	The width of the video image
		height	integer	greater than 0	The height of the video image

Media Type	Description	Property	Property Type	Property Values	Property Description
framerate	fraction	greater or equal 0; default 0/1	The (average) framerate in frames per second. Note that this property does not guarantee in *any* way that it will actually come close to this value. If you need a fixed framerate, please use an element that provides that (such as "videorate"). 0/1 means a variable framerate.		

Media Type	Description	Property	Property Type	Property Values	Property Description
max-framerate	fraction	greater or equal 0; default as framerate	For variable framerates, the maximum framerate that is expected. Only valid when framerate is 0/1.		
views	integer	greater than 0; default 1	The number of views for multiview video. Each buffer contains multiple "GstVideoMeta" buffers that describe each view. Use the frame ID to get access to the different views.		

Media Type	Description	Property	Property Type	Property Values	Property Description
interlace-mode	string	progressive, interleaved, mixed, fields; default progressive	The interlace mode. Extra buffer flags describe the frame and fields.		
chroma-site	string	jpeg, mpeg2, dv; default UNKNOWN	The chroma siting of the video frames.		
colorimetry	string	bt601, bt709, smpte240m; default UNKNOWN	The colorimetry of the video frames.		
pixel-aspect-ratio	fraction	greater than 0; default 1/1	The pixel aspect ratio of the video.		

Media Type	Description	Property	Property Type	Property Values	Property Description
format	string	I420 YV12 YUY2 UYVY AYUV RGBx BGRx xRGB xBGR RGBA BGRA ARGB ABGR RGB BGR Y41B Y42B YVYU Y444 v210 v216 NV12 NV21 GRAY8 GRAY16_LE GRAY16_BE v308 RGB16 BGR16 RGB15 BGR15 UYVP A420 RGB8P YUV9 YVU9 IYU1 ARGB64 AYUV64 r210 I420_10LE I420_10BE I422_10LE I422_10BE	The format of the video. See FourCC definition site (http://www.fourcc.org/) for references and definitions. YUY2, YVYU and UYVY are 4:2:2 packed-pixel, Y41P is 4:1:1 packed-pixel and IYU2 is 4:4:4 packed-pixel. Y42B is 4:2:2 planar, YV12 and I420 are 4:2:0 planar, Y41B is 4:1:1 planar and YUV9 and YVU9 are 4:1:0 planar. Y800 contains Y-samples only (black/white).		

Media Type	Description	Property	Property Type	Property Values	Property Description
All raw video types.					
video/x-raw	Unstructured and uncompressed raw video data.				The properties width, height and format are mandatory.
All encoded video types.					
video/x-3ivx	3ivx video.				There are currently no specific properties defined or needed for this type.
video/x-divx	DivX video.	divxversion	integer	3, 4 or 5	Version of the DivX codec used to encode the stream.
video/x-dv	Digital Video.	systemstream	boolean	FALSE	Indicates that this stream is *not* a system container stream.
video/x-ffv	FFMpeg video.	ffvversion	integer	1	Version of the FFMpeg video codec used to encode the stream.
video/x-h263	H-263 video.	variant	string	itu, lead, microsoft, vdolive, vivo, xirlink	Vendor specific variant of the format. 'itu' is the standard.
		h263version	string	h263, h263p, h263pp	Enhanced versions of the h263 codec.
video/x-h264	H-264 video.	variant	string	itu, videosoft	Vendor specific variant of the format. 'itu' is the standard.
video/x-huffyuv	Huffyuv video.				There are currently no specific properties defined or needed for this type.
video/x-indeo	Indeo video.	indeoversion	integer	3	Version of the Indeo codec used to encode this stream.

Media Type	Description	Property Name	Property Type	Property Values	Property Description
video/x-intel-h263	H-263 video.	variant	string	intel	Vendor specific variant of the format.
video/x-jpeg	Motion-JPEG video.				There are currently no specific properties defined or needed for this type. Note that video/x-jpeg only applies to Motion-JPEG pictures (YUY2 colourspace). RGB colourspace JPEG images are referred to as image/jpeg (JPEG image).
video/mpeg	MPEG video.	mpegversion	integer	1, 2 or 4	Version of the MPEG codec that this stream was encoded with. Note that we have different media types for 3ivx, XviD, DivX and "standard" ISO MPEG-4. This is *not* a good thing and we're fully aware of this. However, we do not have a solution yet.
		systemstream	boolean	FALSE	Indicates that this stream is *not* a system container stream.
video/x-msmpeg	Microsoft MPEG-4 video deviations.	msmpegversion	integer	41, 42 or 43	Version of the MS-MPEG-4-like codec that was used to encode this version. A value of 41 refers to MS MPEG 4.1, 42 to 4.2 and 43 to version 4.3.
video/x-msvideocodec	Microsoft Video 1 (oldish codec).	msvideoversion	integer	1	Version of the codec - always 1.
video/x-pn-realvideo	Realmedia video.	rmversion	integer	1, 2 or 3	Version of the Real Video codec that this stream was encoded with.
video/x-rle	RLE animation format.	layout	string	"microsoft" or "quicktime"	The RLE format inside the Microsoft AVI container has a different byte layout than the RLE format inside Apple's Quicktime container; this property keeps track of the layout.

Media Type	Description	Property	Property Type	Property Values	Property Description
depth	integer	1 to 64	Bit depth of the used palette. This means that the palette that belongs to this format defines 2^depth colors.		
palette_data	GstBuffer		Buffer containing a color palette (in native-endian RGBA) used by this format. The buffer is of size 4*2^depth.		
video/x-svq	Sorensen Video.	svqversion	integer	1 or 3	Version of the Sorensen codec that the stream was encoded with.
video/x-tarkin	Tarkin video.				There are currently no specific properties defined or needed for this type.
video/x-theora	Theora video.				There are currently no specific properties defined or needed for this type.

Media Type	Description	Property Name	Property Type	Property Values	Property Description
video/x-vp3	VP-3 video.				There are currently no specific properties defined or needed for this type. Note that we have different media types for VP-3 and Theora, which is not necessarily a good idea. This could probably be improved.
video/x-wmv	Windows Media Video	wmvversion	integer	1,2 or 3	Version of the WMV codec that the stream was encoded with.
video/x-xvid	XviD video.				There are currently no specific properties defined or needed for this type.
All image types.					
image/gif	Graphics Interchange Format.				There are currently no specific properties defined or needed for this type.
image/jpeg	Joint Picture Expert Group Image.				There are currently no specific properties defined or needed for this type. Note that image/jpeg only applies to RGB-colourspace JPEG images; YUY2-colourspace JPEG pictures are referred to as video/x-jpeg ("Motion JPEG").
image/png	Portable Network Graphics Image.				There are currently no specific properties defined or needed for this type.
image/tiff	Tagged Image File Format.				There are currently no specific properties defined or needed for this type.

Table 16-3. Table of Container Types

Media Type	Description	Property Name	Property Type	Property Values	Property Description
video/x-ms-asf	Advanced Streaming Format (ASF).				There are currently no specific properties defined or needed for this type.
video/x-msvideo	AVI.				There are currently no specific properties defined or needed for this type.

Media Type	Description	Property	Property Type	Property Values	Property Description
video/x-dv	Digital Video.	systemstream	boolean	TRUE	Indicates that this is a container system stream rather than an elementary video stream.
video/x-matroska	Matroska.				There are currently no specific properties defined or needed for this type.
video/mpeg	Motion Pictures Expert Group System Stream.	systemstream	boolean	TRUE	Indicates that this is a container system stream rather than an elementary video stream.
application/ogg	Ogg.				There are currently no specific properties defined or needed for this type.
video/quicktime	Quicktime.				There are currently no specific properties defined or needed for this type.
application/vnd.rn-realmedia	RealMedia.				There are currently no specific properties defined or needed for this type.
audio/x-wav	WAV.				There are currently no specific properties defined or needed for this type.

Table 16-4. Table of Subtitle Types

Media Type	Description	Property	Property Type	Property Values	Property Description
					None defined yet.

Table 16-5. Table of Other Types

Media Type	Description	Property	Property Type	Property Values	Property Description
					None defined yet.

Chapter 17. Events: Seeking, Navigation and More

There are many different event types but only two ways they can travel in the pipeline: downstream or upstream. It is very important to understand how both of these methods work because if one element in the pipeline is not handling them correctly the whole event system of the pipeline is broken. We will try to explain here how these methods work and how elements are supposed to implement them.

17.1. Downstream events

Downstream events are received through the sink pad's event handler, as set using `gst_pad_set_event_function ()` when the pad was created.

Downstream events can travel in two ways: they can be in-band (serialised with the buffer flow) or out-of-band (travelling through the pipeline instantly, possibly not in the same thread as the streaming thread that is processing the buffers, skipping ahead of buffers being processed or queued in the pipeline). The most common downstream events (SEGMENT, CAPS, TAG, EOS) are all serialised with the buffer flow.

Here is a typical event function:

```
static gboolean
gst_my_filter_sink_event (GstPad  *pad, GstObject * parent, GstEvent * event)
{
  GstMyFilter *filter;
  gboolean ret;

  filter = GST_MY_FILTER (parent);
  ...

  switch (GST_EVENT_TYPE (event)) {
    case GST_EVENT_SEGMENT:
      /* maybe save and/or update the current segment (e.g. for output
       * clipping) or convert the event into one in a different format
       * (e.g. BYTES to TIME) or drop it and set a flag to send a segment
       * event in a different format later */
      ret = gst_pad_push_event (filter->src_pad, event);
      break;
    case GST_EVENT_EOS:
      /* end-of-stream, we should close down all stream leftovers here */
      gst_my_filter_stop_processing (filter);
      ret = gst_pad_push_event (filter->src_pad, event);
      break;
    case GST_EVENT_FLUSH_STOP:
      gst_my_filter_clear_temporary_buffers (filter);
```

```
    ret = gst_pad_push_event (filter->src_pad, event);
    break;
  default:
    ret = gst_pad_event_default (pad, parent, event);
    break;
}

...

return ret;
}
```

If your element is chain-based, you will almost always have to implement a sink event function, since that is how you are notified about segments, caps and the end of the stream.

If your element is exclusively loop-based, you may or may not want a sink event function (since the element is driving the pipeline it will know the length of the stream in advance or be notified by the flow return value of `gst_pad_pull_range()`. In some cases even loop-based element may receive events from upstream though (for example audio decoders with an id3demux or apedemux element in front of them, or demuxers that are being fed input from sources that send additional information about the stream in custom events, as DVD sources do).

17.2. Upstream events

Upstream events are generated by an element somewhere downstream in the pipeline (example: a video sink may generate navigation events that informs upstream elements about the current position of the mouse pointer). This may also happen indirectly on request of the application, for example when the application executes a seek on a pipeline this seek request will be passed on to a sink element which will then in turn generate an upstream seek event.

The most common upstream events are seek events, Quality-of-Service (QoS) and reconfigure events.

An upstream event can be sent using the `gst_pad_send_event` function. This function simply call the default event handler of that pad. The default event handler of pads is `gst_pad_event_default`, and it basically sends the event to the peer of the internally linked pad. So upstream events always arrive on the src pad of your element and are handled by the default event handler except if you override that handler to handle it yourself. There are some specific cases where you have to do that :

• If you have multiple sink pads in your element. In that case you will have to decide which one of the sink pads you will send the event to (if not all of them).

• If you need to handle that event locally. For example a navigation event that you will want to convert before sending it upstream, or a QoS event that you want to handle.

The processing you will do in that event handler does not really matter but there are important rules you have to absolutely respect because one broken element event handler is breaking the whole pipeline event handling. Here they are :

• Always handle events you won't handle using the default `gst_pad_event_default` method. This method will depending on the event, forward the event or drop it.

• If you are generating some new event based on the one you received don't forget to gst_event_unref the event you received.

• Event handler function are supposed to return TRUE or FALSE indicating if the event has been handled or not. Never simply return TRUE/FALSE in that handler except if you really know that you have handled that event.

• Remember that the event handler might be called from a different thread than the streaming thread, so make sure you use appropriate locking everywhere.

17.3. All Events Together

In this chapter follows a list of all defined events that are currently being used, plus how they should be used/interpreted. You can check the what type a certain event is using the GST_EVENT_TYPE macro (or if you need a string for debugging purposes you can use GST_EVENT_TYPE_NAME).

In this chapter, we will discuss the following events:

• Stream Start

• Caps

• Segment

• Tag (metadata)

• End of Stream (EOS)

• Table Of Contents

• Gap

• Flush Start

• Flush Stop

• Quality Of Service (QOS)

• Seek Request

• Navigation

For more comprehensive information about events and how they should be used correctly in various circumstances please consult the GStreamer design documentation. This section only gives a general overview.

17.3.1. Stream Start

WRITEME

17.3.2. Caps

The CAPS event contains the format description of the following buffers. See Caps negotiation for more information about negotiation.

17.3.3. Segment

A segment event is sent downstream to announce the range of valid timestamps in the stream and how they should be transformed into running-time and stream-time. A segment event must always be sent before the first buffer of data and after a flush (see above).

The first segment event is created by the element driving the pipeline, like a source operating in push-mode or a demuxer/decoder operating pull-based. This segment event then travels down the pipeline and may be transformed on the way (a decoder, for example, might receive a segment event in BYTES format and might transform this into a segment event in TIMES format based on the average bitrate).

Depending on the element type, the event can simply be forwarded using `gst_pad_event_default ()`, or it should be parsed and a modified event should be sent on. The last is true for demuxers, which generally have a byte-to-time conversion concept. Their input is usually byte-based, so the incoming event will have an offset in byte units (GST_FORMAT_BYTES), too. Elements downstream, however, expect segment events in time units, so that it can be used to synchronize against the pipeline clock. Therefore, demuxers and similar elements should not forward the event, but parse it, free it and send a segment event (in time units, GST_FORMAT_TIME) further downstream.

The segment event is created using the function `gst_event_new_segment ()`. See the API reference and design document for details about its parameters.

Elements parsing this event can use gst_event_parse_segment() to extract the event details. Elements may find the GstSegment API useful to keep track of the current segment (if they want to use it for output clipping, for example).

17.3.4. Tag (metadata)

Tagging events are being sent downstream to indicate the tags as parsed from the stream data. This is currently used to preserve tags during stream transcoding from one format to the other. Tags are discussed extensively in Chapter 22. Most elements will simply forward the event by calling `gst_pad_event_default ()`.

The tag event is created using the function `gst_event_new_tag ()`, but more often elements will send a tag event downstream that will be converted into a message on the bus by sink elements. All of these functions require a filled-in taglist as argument, which they will take ownership of.

Elements parsing this event can use the function `gst_event_parse_tag ()` to acquire the taglist that the event contains.

17.3.5. End of Stream (EOS)

End-of-stream events are sent if the stream that an element sends out is finished. An element receiving this event (from upstream, so it receives it on its sinkpad) will generally just process any buffered data (if there is any) and then forward the event further downstream. The `gst_pad_event_default ()` takes care of all this, so most elements do not need to support this event. Exceptions are elements that explicitly need to close a resource down on EOS, and N-to-1 elements. Note that the stream itself is *not* a resource that should be closed down on EOS! Applications might seek back to a point before EOS and continue playing again.

The EOS event has no properties, which makes it one of the simplest events in GStreamer. It is created using the `gst_event_new_eos ()` function.

It is important to note that *only elements driving the pipeline should ever send an EOS event*. If your element is chain-based, it is not driving the pipeline. Chain-based elements should just return GST_FLOW_EOS from their chain function at the end of the stream (or the configured segment), the upstream element that is driving the pipeline will then take care of sending the EOS event (or alternatively post a SEGMENT_DONE message on the bus depending on the mode of operation). If you are implementing your own source element, you also do not need to ever manually send an EOS event, you should also just return GST_FLOW_EOS in your create or fill function (assuming your element derives from GstBaseSrc or GstPushSrc).

17.3.6. Table Of Contents

WRITEME

17.3.7. Gap

WRITEME

17.3.8. Flush Start

The flush start event is sent downstream (in push mode) or upstream (in pull mode) if all buffers and caches in the pipeline should be emptied. "Queue" elements will empty their internal list of buffers when they receive this event, for example. File sink elements (e.g. "filesink") will flush the kernel-to-disk cache (`fdatasync ()` or `fflush ()`) when they receive this event. Normally, elements receiving this event will simply just forward it, since most filter or filter-like elements don't have an internal cache of data. `gst_pad_event_default ()` does just that, so for most elements, it is enough to forward the event using the default event handler.

As a side-effect of flushing all data from the pipeline, this event unblocks the streaming thread by making all pads reject data until they receive a Flush Stop signal (elements trying to push data will get a FLUSHING flow return and stop processing data).

The flush-start event is created with the `gst_event_new_flush_start ()`. Like the EOS event, it has no properties. This event is usually only created by elements driving the pipeline, like source elements operating in push-mode or pull-range based demuxers/decoders.

17.3.9. Flush Stop

The flush-stop event is sent by an element driving the pipeline after a flush-start and tells pads and elements downstream that they should accept events and buffers again (there will be at least a SEGMENT event before any buffers first though).

If your element keeps temporary caches of stream data, it should clear them when it receives a FLUSH-STOP event (and also whenever its chain function receives a buffer with the DISCONT flag set).

The flush-stop event is created with `gst_event_new_flush_stop ()`. It has one parameter that controls if the running-time of the pipeline should be reset to 0 or not. Normally after a flushing seek, the running_time is set back to 0.

17.3.10. Quality Of Service (QOS)

The QOS event contains a report about the current real-time performance of the stream. See more info in Chapter 19.

17.3.11. Seek Request

Seek events are meant to request a new stream position to elements. This new position can be set in several formats (time, bytes or "default units" [a term indicating frames for video, channel-independent samples for audio, etc.]). Seeking can be done with respect to the end-of-file or start-of-file, and usually happens in upstream direction (downstream seeking is done by sending a SEGMENT event with the appropriate offsets for elements that support that, like filesink).

Elements receiving seek events should, depending on the element type, either just forward it upstream (filters, decoders), change the format in which the event is given and then forward it (demuxers), or handle the event by changing the file pointer in their internal stream resource (file sources, demuxers/decoders driving the pipeline in pull-mode) or something else.

Seek events are built up using positions in specified formats (time, bytes, units). They are created using the function `gst_event_new_seek ()`. Note that many plugins do not support seeking from the end of the stream. An element not driving the pipeline and forwarding a seek request should not assume that the seek succeeded or actually happened, it should operate based on the SEGMENT events it receives.

Elements parsing this event can do this using `gst_event_parse_seek()`.

17.3.12. Navigation

Navigation events are sent upstream by video sinks to inform upstream elements of where the mouse pointer is, if and where mouse pointer clicks have happened, or if keys have been pressed or released.

All this information is contained in the event structure which can be obtained with `gst_event_get_structure ()`.

Check out the navigationtest element in gst-plugins-good for an idea how to extract navigation information from this event.

Chapter 18. Clocking

When playing complex media, each sound and video sample must be played in a specific order at a specific time. For this purpose, GStreamer provides a synchronization mechanism.

18.1. Clocks

Time in GStreamer is defined as the value returned from a particular `GstClock` object from the method `gst_clock_get_time ()`.

In a typical computer, there are many sources that can be used as a time source, e.g., the system time, soundcards, CPU performance counters, ... For this reason, there are many `GstClock` implementations available in GStreamer. The clock time doesn't always start from 0 or from some known value. Some clocks start counting from some known start date, other clocks start counting since last reboot, etc...

As clocks return an absolute measure of time, they are not usually used directly. Instead, differences between two clock times are used to measure elapsed time according to a clock.

18.2. Clock running-time

A clock returns the **absolute-time** according to that clock with `gst_clock_get_time ()`. From the absolute-time is a **running-time** calculated, which is simply the difference between a previous snapshot of the absolute-time called the **base-time**. So:

running-time = absolute-time - base-time

A GStreamer `GstPipeline` object maintains a `GstClock` object and a base-time when it goes to the PLAYING state. The pipeline gives a handle to the selected `GstClock` to each element in the pipeline along with selected base-time. The pipeline will select a base-time in such a way that the running-time reflects the total time spent in the PLAYING state. As a result, when the pipeline is PAUSED, the running-time stands still.

Because all objects in the pipeline have the same clock and base-time, they can thus all calculate the running-time according to the pipeline clock.

18.3. Buffer running-time

To calculate a buffer running-time, we need a buffer timestamp and the SEGMENT event that preceded the buffer. First we can convert the SEGMENT event into a `GstSegment` object and then we can use the `gst_segment_to_running_time ()` function to perform the calculation of the buffer running-time.

Synchronization is now a matter of making sure that a buffer with a certain running-time is played when the clock reaches the same running-time. Usually this task is done by sink elements. Sink also have to take into account the latency configured in the pipeline and add this to the buffer running-time before synchronizing to the pipeline clock.

18.4. Obligations of each element.

Let us clarify the contract between GStreamer and each element in the pipeline.

18.4.1. Non-live source elements

Non-live source elements must place a timestamp in each buffer that they deliver when this is possible. They must choose the timestamps and the values of the SEGMENT event in such a way that the running-time of the buffer starts from 0.

Some sources, such as filesrc, is not able to generate timestamps on all buffers. It can and must however create a timestamp on the first buffer (with a running-time of 0).

The source then pushes out the SEGMENT event followed by the timestamped buffers.

18.4.2. Live source elements

Live source elements must place a timestamp in each buffer that they deliver. They must choose the timestamps and the values of the SEGMENT event in such a way that the running-time of the buffer matches exactly the running-time of the pipeline clock when the first byte in the buffer was captured.

18.4.3. Parser/Decoder/Encoder elements

Parser/Decoder elements must use the incoming timestamps and transfer those to the resulting output buffers. They are allowed to interpolate or reconstruct timestamps on missing input buffers when they can.

18.4.4. Demuxer elements

Demuxer elements can usually set the timestamps stored inside the media file onto the outgoing buffers. They need to make sure that outgoing buffers that are to be played at the same time have the same running-time. Demuxers also need to take into account the incoming timestamps on buffers and use that to calculate an offset on the outgoing buffer timestamps.

18.4.5. Muxer elements

Muxer elements should use the incoming buffer running-time to mux the different streams together. They should copy the incoming running-time to the outgoing buffers.

18.4.6. Sink elements

If the element is intended to emit samples at a specific time (real time playing), the element should require a clock, and thus implement the method `set_clock`.

The sink should then make sure that the sample with running-time is played exactly when the pipeline clock reaches that running-time + latency. Some elements might use the clock API such as `gst_clock_id_wait()` to perform this action. Other sinks might need to use other means of scheduling timely playback of the data.

Chapter 19. Quality Of Service (QoS)

Quality of Service in GStreamer is about measuring and adjusting the real-time performance of a pipeline. The real-time performance is always measured relative to the pipeline clock and typically happens in the sinks when they synchronize buffers against the clock.

When buffers arrive late in the sink, i.e. when their running-time is smaller than that of the clock, we say that the pipeline is having a quality of service problem. These are a few possible reasons:

- High CPU load, there is not enough CPU power to handle the stream, causing buffers to arrive late in the sink.

- Network problems

- Other resource problems such as disk load, memory bottlenecks etc

The measurements result in QOS events that aim to adjust the datarate in one or more upstream elements. Two types of adjustments can be made:

- Short time "emergency" corrections based on latest observation in the sinks.

  Long term rate corrections based on trends observed in the sinks.

It is also possible for the application to artificially introduce delay between synchronized buffers, this is called throttling. It can be used to limit or reduce the framerate, for example.

19.1. Measuring QoS

Elements that synchronize buffers on the pipeline clock will usually measure the current QoS. They will also need to keep some statistics in order to generate the QOS event.

For each buffer that arrives in the sink, the element needs to calculate how late or how early it was. This is called the jitter. Negative jitter values mean that the buffer was early, positive values mean that the buffer was late. the jitter value gives an indication of how early/late a buffer was.

A synchronizing element will also need to calculate how much time elapsed between receiving two consecutive buffers. We call this the processing time because that is the amount of time it takes for the upstream element to produce/process the buffer. We can compare this processing time to the duration of the buffer to have a measurement of how fast upstream can produce data, called the proportion. If, for example, upstream can produce a buffer in 0.5 seconds of 1 second long, it is operating at twice the required speed. If, on the other hand, it takes 2 seconds to produce a buffer with 1 seconds worth of data, upstream is producing buffers too slow and we won't be able to keep synchronization. Usually, a running average is kept of the proportion.

A synchronizing element also needs to measure its own performance in order to figure out if the performance problem is upstream of itself.

These measurements are used to construct a QOS event that is sent upstream. Note that a QoS event is sent for each buffer that arrives in the sink.

19.2. Handling QoS

An element will have to install an event function on its source pads in order to receive QOS events. Usually, the element will need to store the value of the QOS event and use them in the data processing function. The element will need to use a lock to protect these QoS values as shown in the example below. Also make sure to pass the QoS event upstream.

```
[...]

case GST_EVENT_QOS:
{
  GstQOSType type;
  gdouble proportion;
  GstClockTimeDiff diff;
  GstClockTime timestamp;

  gst_event_parse_qos (event, &type, &proportion, &diff, &timestamp);

  GST_OBJECT_LOCK (decoder);
  priv->qos_proportion = proportion;
  priv->qos_timestamp = timestamp;
  priv->qos_diff = diff;
  GST_OBJECT_UNLOCK (decoder);

  res = gst_pad_push_event (decoder->sinkpad, event);
  break;
}

[...]
```

With the QoS values, there are two types of corrections that an element can do:

19.2.1. Short term correction

The timestamp and the jitter value in the QOS event can be used to perform a short term correction. If the jitter is positive, the previous buffer arrived late and we can be sure that a buffer with a timestamp < timestamp + jitter is also going to be late. We can thus drop all buffers with a timestamp less than timestamp + jitter.

If the buffer duration is known, a better estimation for the next likely timestamp as: timestamp + 2 * jitter + duration.

A possible algorithm typically looks like this:

```
[...]

GST_OBJECT_LOCK (dec);
qos_proportion = priv->qos_proportion;
qos_timestamp = priv->qos_timestamp;
qos_diff = priv->qos_diff;
GST_OBJECT_UNLOCK (dec);

/* calculate the earliest valid timestamp */
if (G_LIKELY (GST_CLOCK_TIME_IS_VALID (qos_timestamp))) {
  if (G_UNLIKELY (qos_diff > 0)) {
    earliest_time = qos_timestamp + 2 * qos_diff + frame_duration;
  } else {
    earliest_time = qos_timestamp + qos_diff;
  }
} else {
  earliest_time = GST_CLOCK_TIME_NONE;
}

/* compare earliest_time to running-time of next buffer */
if (earliest_time > timestamp)
  goto drop_buffer;

[...]
```

19.2.2. Long term correction

Long term corrections are a bit more difficult to perform. They rely on the value of the proportion in the QOS event. Elements should reduce the amount of resources they consume by the proportion field in the QoS message.

Here are some possible strategies to achieve this:

- Permanently dropping frames or reducing the CPU or bandwidth requirements of the element. Some decoders might be able to skip decoding of B frames.

- Switch to lower quality processing or reduce the algorithmic complexity. Care should be taken that this doesn't introduce disturbing visual or audible glitches.

- Switch to a lower quality source to reduce network bandwidth.

- Assign more CPU cycles to critical parts of the pipeline. This could, for example, be done by increasing the thread priority.

In all cases, elements should be prepared to go back to their normal processing rate when the proportion member in the QOS event approaches the ideal proportion of 1.0 again.

19.3. Throttling

Elements synchronizing to the clock should expose a property to configure them in throttle mode. In throttle mode, the time distance between buffers is kept to a configurable throttle interval. This means that effectively the buffer rate is limited to 1 buffer per throttle interval. This can be used to limit the framerate, for example.

When an element is configured in throttling mode (this is usually only implemented on sinks) it should produce QoS events upstream with the jitter field set to the throttle interval. This should instruct upstream elements to skip or drop the remaining buffers in the configured throttle interval.

The proportion field is set to the desired slowdown needed to get the desired throttle interval. Implementations can use the QoS Throttle type, the proportion and the jitter member to tune their implementations.

The default sink base class, has the "throttle-time" property for this feature. You can test this with:
gst-launch-1.0 videotestsrc ! xvimagesink throttle-time=500000000

19.4. QoS Messages

In addition to the QOS events that are sent between elements in the pipeline, there are also QOS messages posted on the pipeline bus to inform the application of QoS decisions. The QOS message contains the timestamps of when something was dropped along with the amount of dropped vs processed items. Elements must post a QOS message under these conditions:

- The element dropped a buffer because of QoS reasons.

- An element changes its processing strategy because of QoS reasons (quality). This could include a decoder that decides to drop every B frame to increase its processing speed or an effect element switching to a lower quality algorithm.

Chapter 20. Supporting Dynamic Parameters

Warning, this part describes 0.10 and is outdated.

Sometimes object properties are not powerful enough to control the parameters that affect the behaviour of your element. When this is the case you can mark these parameters as being Controllable. Aware applications can use the controller subsystem to dynamically adjust the property values over time.

20.1. Getting Started

The controller subsystem is contained within the `gstcontroller` library. You need to include the header in your element's source file:

```
...
#include <gst/gst.h>
#include <gst/controller/gstcontroller.h>
...
```

Even though the `gstcontroller` library may be linked into the host application, you should make sure it is initialized in your `plugin_init` function:

```
static gboolean
plugin_init (GstPlugin *plugin)
{
  ...
  /* initialize library */
  gst_controller_init (NULL, NULL);
  ...
}
```

It makes no sense for all GObject parameter to be real-time controlled. Therefore the next step is to mark controllable parameters. This is done by using the special flag GST_PARAM_CONTROLLABLE. when setting up GObject params in the `_class_init` method.

```
g_object_class_install_property (gobject_class, PROP_FREQ,
    g_param_spec_double ("freq", "Frequency", "Frequency of test signal",
        0.0, 20000.0, 440.0,
        G_PARAM_READWRITE | GST_PARAM_CONTROLLABLE | G_PARAM_STATIC_STRINGS));
```

20.2. The Data Processing Loop

In the last section we learned how to mark GObject params as controllable. Application developers can then queue parameter changes for these parameters. The approach the controller subsystem takes is to make plugins responsible for pulling the changes in. This requires just one action:

```
gst_object_sync_values(element,timestamp);
```

This call makes all parameter-changes for the given timestamp active by adjusting the GObject properties of the element. Its up to the element to determine the synchronisation rate.

20.2.1. The Data Processing Loop for Video Elements

For video processing elements it is the best to synchronise for every frame. That means one would add the `gst_object_sync_values()` call described in the previous section to the data processing function of the element.

20.2.2. The Data Processing Loop for Audio Elements

For audio processing elements the case is not as easy as for video processing elements. The problem here is that audio has a much higher rate. For PAL video one will e.g. process 25 full frames per second, but for standard audio it will be 44100 samples. It is rarely useful to synchronise controllable parameters that often. The easiest solution is also to have just one synchronisation call per buffer processing. This makes the control-rate depend on the buffer size.

Elements that need a specific control-rate need to break their data processing loop to synchronise every n-samples.

Chapter 21. Interfaces

Previously, in the chapter Adding Properties, we have introduced the concept of GObject properties of controlling an element's behaviour. This is very powerful, but it has two big disadvantages: first of all, it is too generic, and second, it isn't dynamic.

The first disadvantage is related to the customizability of the end-user interface that will be built to control the element. Some properties are more important than others. Some integer properties are better shown in a spin-button widget, whereas others would be better represented by a slider widget. Such things are not possible because the UI has no actual meaning in the application. A UI widget that represents a bitrate property is the same as a UI widget that represents the size of a video, as long as both are of the same GParamSpec type. Another problem, is that things like parameter grouping, function grouping, or parameter coupling are not really possible.

The second problem with parameters are that they are not dynamic. In many cases, the allowed values for a property are not fixed, but depend on things that can only be detected at runtime. The names of inputs for a TV card in a video4linux source element, for example, can only be retrieved from the kernel driver when we've opened the device; this only happens when the element goes into the READY state. This means that we cannot create an enum property type to show this to the user.

The solution to those problems is to create very specialized types of controls for certain often-used controls. We use the concept of interfaces to achieve this. The basis of this all is the glib GTypeInterface type. For each case where we think it's useful, we've created interfaces which can be implemented by elements at their own will.

One important note: interfaces do *not* replace properties. Rather, interfaces should be built *next to* properties. There are two important reasons for this. First of all, properties can be more easily introspected. Second, properties can be specified on the commandline (gst-launch).

21.1. How to Implement Interfaces

Implementing interfaces is initiated in the _get_type () of your element. You can register one or more interfaces after having registered the type itself. Some interfaces have dependencies on other interfaces or can only be registered by certain types of elements. You will be notified of doing that wrongly when using the element: it will quit with failed assertions, which will explain what went wrong. If it does, you need to register support for *that* interface before registering support for the interface that you're wanting to support. The example below explains how to add support for a simple interface with no further dependencies.

```
static void gst_my_filter_some_interface_init (GstSomeInterface *iface);

GType
gst_my_filter_get_type (void)
```

```
{
  static GType my_filter_type = 0;

  if (!my_filter_type) {
    static const GTypeInfo my_filter_info = {
      sizeof (GstMyFilterClass),
      NULL,
      NULL,
      (GClassInitFunc) gst_my_filter_class_init,
      NULL,
      NULL,
      sizeof (GstMyFilter),
      0,
      (GInstanceInitFunc) gst_my_filter_init
    };
    static const GInterfaceInfo some_interface_info = {
      (GInterfaceInitFunc) gst_my_filter_some_interface_init,
      NULL,
      NULL
    };

    my_filter_type =
g_type_register_static (GST_TYPE_ELEMENT,
"GstMyFilter",
&my_filter_info, 0);
    g_type_add_interface_static (my_filter_type,
 GST_TYPE_SOME_INTERFACE,
                                  &some_interface_info);
  }

  return my_filter_type;
}

static void
gst_my_filter_some_interface_init (GstSomeInterface *iface)
{
  /* here, you would set virtual function pointers in the interface */
}
```

Or more conveniently:

```
static void gst_my_filter_some_interface_init (GstSomeInterface *iface);

G_DEFINE_TYPE_WITH_CODE (GstMyFilter, gst_my_filter,GST_TYPE_ELEMENT,
    G_IMPLEMENT_INTERFACE (GST_TYPE_SOME_INTERFACE,
           gst_my_filter_some_interface_init));
```

21.2. URI interface

WRITEME

21.3. Color Balance Interface

WRITEME

21.4. Video Overlay Interface

The #GstVideoOverlay interface is used for 2 main purposes :

- To get a grab on the Window where the video sink element is going to render. This is achieved by either being informed about the Window identifier that the video sink element generated, or by forcing the video sink element to use a specific Window identifier for rendering.
- To force a redrawing of the latest video frame the video sink element displayed on the Window. Indeed if the #GstPipeline is in #GST_STATE_PAUSED state, moving the Window around will damage its content. Application developers will want to handle the Expose events themselves and force the video sink element to refresh the Window's content.

A plugin drawing video output in a video window will need to have that window at one stage or another. Passive mode simply means that no window has been given to the plugin before that stage, so the plugin created the window by itself. In that case the plugin is responsible of destroying that window when it's not needed any more and it has to tell the applications that a window has been created so that the application can use it. This is done using the `have-window-handle` message that can be posted from the plugin with the `gst_video_overlay_got_window_handle` method.

As you probably guessed already active mode just means sending a video window to the plugin so that video output goes there. This is done using the `gst_video_overlay_set_window_handle` method.

It is possible to switch from one mode to another at any moment, so the plugin implementing this interface has to handle all cases. There are only 2 methods that plugins writers have to implement and they most probably look like that :

```
static void
gst_my_filter_set_window_handle (GstVideoOverlay *overlay, guintptr handle)
{
  GstMyFilter *my_filter = GST_MY_FILTER (overlay);

  if (my_filter->window)
```

```
      gst_my_filter_destroy_window (my_filter->window);

  my_filter->window = handle;
}

static void
gst_my_filter_xoverlay_init (GstVideoOverlayClass *iface)
{
  iface->set_window_handle = gst_my_filter_set_window_handle;
}
```

You will also need to use the interface methods to post messages when needed such as when receiving a CAPS event where you will know the video geometry and maybe create the window.

```
static MyFilterWindow *
gst_my_filter_window_create (GstMyFilter *my_filter, gint width, gint height)
{
  MyFilterWindow *window = g_new (MyFilterWindow, 1);
  ...
  gst_video_overlay_got_window_handle (GST_VIDEO_OVERLAY (my_filter), window->win);
}

/* called from the event handler for CAPS events */
static gboolean
gst_my_filter_sink_set_caps (GstMyFilter *my_filter, GstCaps *caps)
{
  gint width, height;
  gboolean ret;
  ...
  ret = gst_structure_get_int (structure, "width", &width);
  ret &= gst_structure_get_int (structure, "height", &height);
  if (!ret) return FALSE;

  gst_video_overlay_prepare_window_handle (GST_VIDEO_OVERLAY (my_filter));

  if (!my_filter->window)
    my_filter->window = gst_my_filter_create_window (my_filter, width, height);

  ...
}
```

21.5. Navigation Interface

WRITEME

Chapter 22. Tagging (Metadata and Streaminfo)

22.1. Overview

Tags are pieces of information stored in a stream that are not the content itself, but they rather *describe* the content. Most media container formats support tagging in one way or another. Ogg uses VorbisComment for this, MP3 uses ID3, AVI and WAV use RIFF's INFO list chunk, etc. GStreamer provides a general way for elements to read tags from the stream and expose this to the user. The tags (at least the metadata) will be part of the stream inside the pipeline. The consequence of this is that transcoding of files from one format to another will automatically preserve tags, as long as the input and output format elements both support tagging.

Tags are separated in two categories in GStreamer, even though applications won't notice anything of this. The first are called *metadata*, the second are called *streaminfo*. Metadata are tags that describe the non-technical parts of stream content. They can be changed without needing to re-encode the stream completely. Examples are "author", "title" or "album". The container format might still need to be re-written for the tags to fit in, though. Streaminfo, on the other hand, are tags that describe the stream contents technically. To change them, the stream needs to be re-encoded. Examples are "codec" or "bitrate". Note that some container formats (like ID3) store various streaminfo tags as metadata in the file container, which means that they can be changed so that they don't match the content in the file any more. Still, they are called metadata because *technically*, they can be changed without re-encoding the whole stream, even though that makes them invalid. Files with such metadata tags will have the same tag twice: once as metadata, once as streaminfo.

There is no special name for tag reading elements in GStreamer. There are specialised elements (e.g. id3demux) that do nothing besides tag reading, but any GStreamer element may extract tags while processing data, and most decoders, demuxers and parsers do.

A tag writer is called `TagSetter` (../../gstreamer/html/GstTagSetter.html). An element supporting both can be used in a tag editor for quick tag changing (note: in-place tag editing is still poorly supported at the time of writing and usually requires tag extraction/stripping and remuxing of the stream with new tags).

22.2. Reading Tags from Streams

The basic object for tags is a `GstTagList` (../../gstreamer/html/GstTagList.html). An element that is reading tags from a stream should create an empty taglist and fill this with individual tags. Empty tag lists can be created with `gst_tag_list_new ()`. Then, the element can fill the list using `gst_tag_list_add ()` or `gst_tag_list_add_values ()`. Note that elements often read metadata as strings, but the values in the taglist might not necessarily be strings - they need to be of the type the tag was registered as (the API documentation for each predefined tag should contain the type).

Be sure to use functions like `gst_value_transform ()` to make sure that your data is of the right type. After data reading, you can send the tags downstream with the TAG event. When the TAG event reaches the sink, it will post the TAG message on the pipeline's GstBus for the application to pick up.

We currently require the core to know the GType of tags before they are being used, so all tags must be registered first. You can add new tags to the list of known tags using `gst_tag_register ()`. If you think the tag will be useful in more cases than just your own element, it might be a good idea to add it to `gsttag.c` instead. That's up to you to decide. If you want to do it in your own element, it's easiest to register the tag in one of your class init functions, preferably `_class_init ()`.

```
static void
gst_my_filter_class_init (GstMyFilterClass *klass)
{
[..]
  gst_tag_register ("my_tag_name", GST_TAG_FLAG_META,
    G_TYPE_STRING,
    _("my own tag"),
    _("a tag that is specific to my own element"),
    NULL);
[..]
}
```

22.3. Writing Tags to Streams

Tag writers are the opposite of tag readers. Tag writers only take metadata tags into account, since that's the only type of tags that have to be written into a stream. Tag writers can receive tags in three ways: internal, application and pipeline. Internal tags are tags read by the element itself, which means that the tag writer is - in that case - a tag reader, too. Application tags are tags provided to the element via the TagSetter interface (which is just a layer). Pipeline tags are tags provided to the element from within the pipeline. The element receives such tags via the GST_EVENT_TAG event, which means that tags writers should implement an event handler. The tag writer is responsible for combining all these three into one list and writing them to the output stream.

The example below will receive tags from both application and pipeline, combine them and write them to the output stream. It implements the tag setter so applications can set tags, and retrieves pipeline tags from incoming events.

Warning, this example is outdated and doesn't work with the 1.0 version of GStreamer anymore.

```
GType
gst_my_filter_get_type (void)
{
```

```
[..]
    static const GInterfaceInfo tag_setter_info = {
      NULL,
      NULL,
      NULL
    };
[..]
    g_type_add_interface_static (my_filter_type,
 GST_TYPE_TAG_SETTER,
 &tag_setter_info);
[..]
}

static void
gst_my_filter_init (GstMyFilter *filter)
{
[..]
}

/*
 * Write one tag.
 */

static void
gst_my_filter_write_tag (const GstTagList *taglist,
 const gchar      *tagname,
 gpointer          data)
{
  GstMyFilter *filter = GST_MY_FILTER (data);
  GstBuffer *buffer;
  guint num_values = gst_tag_list_get_tag_size (list, tag_name), n;
  const GValue *from;
  GValue to = { 0 };

  g_value_init (&to, G_TYPE_STRING);

  for (n = 0; n < num_values; n++) {
    guint8 * data;
    gsize size;

    from = gst_tag_list_get_value_index (taglist, tagname, n);
    g_value_transform (from, &to);

    data = g_strdup_printf ("%s:%s", tagname,
g_value_get_string (&to));
    size = strlen (data);

    buf = gst_buffer_new_wrapped (data, size);
    gst_pad_push (filter->srcpad, buf);
  }

  g_value_unset (&to);
}
```

```
static void
gst_my_filter_task_func (GstElement *element)
{
  GstMyFilter *filter = GST_MY_FILTER (element);
  GstTagSetter *tagsetter = GST_TAG_SETTER (element);
  GstData *data;
  GstEvent *event;
  gboolean eos = FALSE;
  GstTagList *taglist = gst_tag_list_new ();

  while (!eos) {
    data = gst_pad_pull (filter->sinkpad);

    /* We're not very much interested in data right now */
    if (GST_IS_BUFFER (data))
      gst_buffer_unref (GST_BUFFER (data));
    event = GST_EVENT (data);

    switch (GST_EVENT_TYPE (event)) {
      case GST_EVENT_TAG:
        gst_tag_list_insert (taglist, gst_event_tag_get_list (event),
     GST_TAG_MERGE_PREPEND);
        gst_event_unref (event);
        break;
      case GST_EVENT_EOS:
        eos = TRUE;
        gst_event_unref (event);
        break;
      default:
        gst_pad_event_default (filter->sinkpad, event);
        break;
    }
  }

  /* merge tags with the ones retrieved from the application */
  if ((gst_tag_setter_get_tag_list (tagsetter)) {
    gst_tag_list_insert (taglist,
 gst_tag_setter_get_tag_list (tagsetter),
 gst_tag_setter_get_tag_merge_mode (tagsetter));
  }

  /* write tags */
  gst_tag_list_foreach (taglist, gst_my_filter_write_tag, filter);

  /* signal EOS */
  gst_pad_push (filter->srcpad, gst_event_new (GST_EVENT_EOS));
}
```

Note that normally, elements would not read the full stream before processing tags. Rather, they would read from each sinkpad until they've received data (since tags usually come in before the first data buffer) and process that.

IV. Creating special element types

By now, we have looked at pretty much any feature that can be embedded into a GStreamer element. Most of this has been fairly low-level and given deep insights in how GStreamer works internally. Fortunately, GStreamer contains some easier-to-use interfaces to create such elements. In order to do that, we will look closer at the element types for which GStreamer provides base classes (sources, sinks and transformation elements). We will also look closer at some types of elements that require no specific coding such as scheduling-interaction or data passing, but rather require specific pipeline control (e.g. N-to-1 elements and managers).

Chapter 23. Pre-made base classes

So far, we've been looking at low-level concepts of creating any type of GStreamer element. Now, let's assume that all you want is to create an simple audiosink that works exactly the same as, say, "esdsink", or a filter that simply normalizes audio volume. Such elements are very general in concept and since they do nothing special, they should be easier to code than to provide your own scheduler activation functions and doing complex caps negotiation. For this purpose, GStreamer provides base classes that simplify some types of elements. Those base classes will be discussed in this chapter.

23.1. Writing a sink

Sinks are special elements in GStreamer. This is because sink elements have to take care of *preroll*, which is the process that takes care that elements going into the GST_STATE_PAUSED state will have buffers ready after the state change. The result of this is that such elements can start processing data immediately after going into the GST_STATE_PLAYING state, without requiring to take some time to initialize outputs or set up decoders; all that is done already before the state-change to GST_STATE_PAUSED successfully completes.

Preroll, however, is a complex process that would require the same code in many elements. Therefore, sink elements can derive from the GstBaseSink base-class, which does preroll and a few other utility functions automatically. The derived class only needs to implement a bunch of virtual functions and will work automatically.

The base class implement much of the synchronization logic that a sink has to perform.

The GstBaseSink base-class specifies some limitations on elements, though:

- It requires that the sink only has one sinkpad. Sink elements that need more than one sinkpad, must make a manager element with multiple GstBaseSink elements inside.

Sink elements can derive from GstBaseSink using the usual GObject convenience macro G_DEFINE_TYPE ():

```
G_DEFINE_TYPE (GstMySink, gst_my_sink, GST_TYPE_BASE_SINK);

[..]

static void
gst_my_sink_class_init (GstMySinkClass * klass)
{
  klass->set_caps = [..];
  klass->render = [..];
[..]
}
```

The advantages of deriving from `GstBaseSink` are numerous:

• Derived implementations barely need to be aware of preroll, and do not need to know anything about the technical implementation requirements of preroll. The base-class does all the hard work.

Less code to write in the derived class, shared code (and thus shared bugfixes).

There are also specialized base classes for audio and video, let's look at those a bit.

23.1.1. Writing an audio sink

Essentially, audio sink implementations are just a special case of a general sink. An audio sink has the added complexity that it needs to schedule playback of samples. It must match the clock selected in the pipeline against the clock of the audio device and calculate and compensate for drift and jitter.

There are two audio base classes that you can choose to derive from, depending on your needs: `GstAudioBasesink` and `GstAudioSink`. The audiobasesink provides full control over how synchronization and scheduling is handled, by using a ringbuffer that the derived class controls and provides. The audiosink base-class is a derived class of the audiobasesink, implementing a standard ringbuffer implementing default synchronization and providing a standard audio-sample clock. Derived classes of this base class merely need to provide a `_open ()`, `_close ()` and a `_write ()` function implementation, and some optional functions. This should suffice for many sound-server output elements and even most interfaces. More demanding audio systems, such as Jack, would want to implement the `GstAudioBaseSink` base-class.

The `GstAudioBaseSink` has little to no limitations and should fit virtually every implementation, but is hard to implement. The `GstAudioSink`, on the other hand, only fits those systems with a simple `open ()` / `close ()` / `write ()` API (which practically means pretty much all of them), but has the advantage that it is a lot easier to implement. The benefits of this second base class are large:

• Automatic synchronization, without any code in the derived class.

• Also automatically provides a clock, so that other sinks (e.g. in case of audio/video playback) are synchronized.

• Features can be added to all audiosinks by making a change in the base class, which makes maintenance easy.

• Derived classes require only three small functions, plus some `GObject` boilerplate code.

In addition to implementing the audio base-class virtual functions, derived classes can (should) also implement the `GstBaseSink set_caps ()` and `get_caps ()` virtual functions for negotiation.

23.1.2. Writing a video sink

Writing a videosink can be done using the `GstVideoSink` base-class, which derives from `GstBaseSink` internally. Currently, it does nothing yet but add another compile dependency, so derived classes will need to implement all base-sink virtual functions. When they do this correctly, this will have some positive effects on the end user experience with the videosink:

• Because of preroll (and the `preroll ()` virtual function), it is possible to display a video frame already when going into the GST_STATE_PAUSED state.

• By adding new features to `GstVideoSink`, it will be possible to add extensions to videosinks that affect all of them, but only need to be coded once, which is a huge maintenance benefit.

23.2. Writing a source

In the previous part, particularly Providing random access, we have learned that some types of elements can provide random access. This applies most definitely to source elements reading from a randomly seekable location, such as file sources. However, other source elements may be better described as a live source element, such as a camera source, an audio card source and such; those are not seekable and do not provide byte-exact access. For all such use cases, GStreamer provides two base classes: `GstBaseSrc` for the basic source functionality, and `GstPushSrc`, which is a non-byte exact source base-class. The pushsource base class itself derives from basesource as well, and thus all statements about the basesource apply to the pushsource, too.

The basesrc class does several things automatically for derived classes, so they no longer have to worry about it:

• Fixes to `GstBaseSrc` apply to all derived classes automatically.

• Automatic pad activation handling, and task-wrapping in case we get assigned to start a task ourselves.

The `GstBaseSrc` may not be suitable for all cases, though; it has limitations:

• There is one and only one sourcepad. Source elements requiring multiple sourcepads must implement a manager bin and use multiple source elements internally or make a manager element that uses a source element and a demuxer inside.

It is possible to use special memory, such as X server memory pointers or `mmap ()`'ed memory areas, as data pointers in buffers returned from the `create()` virtual function.

23.2.1. Writing an audio source

An audio source is nothing more but a special case of a pushsource. Audio sources would be anything that reads audio, such as a source reading from a soundserver, a kernel interface (such as ALSA) or a test sound / signal generator. GStreamer provides two base classes, similar to the two audiosinks described in Writing an audio sink; one is ringbuffer-based, and requires the derived class to take care of its own scheduling, synchronization and such. The other is based on this `GstAudioBaseSrc` and is called `GstAudioSrc`, and provides a simple `open ()`, `close ()` and `read ()` interface, which is rather simple to implement and will suffice for most soundserver sources and audio interfaces (e.g. ALSA or OSS) out there.

The `GstAudioSrc` base-class has several benefits for derived classes, on top of the benefits of the `GstPushSrc` base-class that it is based on:

- Does syncronization and provides a clock.

- New features can be added to it and will apply to all derived classes automatically.

23.3. Writing a transformation element

A third base-class that GStreamer provides is the `GstBaseTransform`. This is a base class for elements with one sourcepad and one sinkpad which act as a filter of some sort, such as volume changing, audio resampling, audio format conversion, and so on and so on. There is quite a lot of bookkeeping that such elements need to do in order for things such as buffer allocation forwarding, passthrough, in-place processing and such to all work correctly. This base class does all that for you, so that you just need to do the actual processing.

Since the `GstBaseTransform` is based on the 1-to-1 model for filters, it may not apply well to elements such as decoders, which may have to parse properties from the stream. Also, it will not work for elements requiring more than one sourcepad or sinkpad.

Chapter 24. Writing a Demuxer or Parser

Demuxers are the 1-to-N elements that need very special care. They are responsible for timestamping raw, unparsed data into elementary video or audio streams, and there are many things that you can optimize or do wrong. Here, several culprits will be mentioned and common solutions will be offered. Parsers are demuxers with only one source pad. Also, they only cut the stream into buffers, they don't touch the data otherwise.

As mentioned previously in Caps negotiation, demuxers should use fixed caps, since their data type will not change.

As discussed in Different scheduling modes, demuxer elements can be written in multiple ways:

- They can be the driving force of the pipeline, by running their own task. This works particularly well for elements that need random access, for example an AVI demuxer.

- They can also run in push-based mode, which means that an upstream element drives the pipeline. This works particularly well for streams that may come from network, such as Ogg.

In addition, audio parsers with one output can, in theory, also be written in random access mode. Although simple playback will mostly work if your element only accepts one mode, it may be required to implement multiple modes to work in combination with all sorts of applications, such as editing. Also, performance may become better if you implement multiple modes. See Different scheduling modes to see how an element can accept multiple scheduling modes.

Chapter 25. Writing a N-to-1 Element or Muxer

N-to-1 elements have been previously mentioned and discussed in both Chapter 12 and in Different scheduling modes. The main noteworthy thing about N-to-1 elements is that each pad is push-based in its own thread, and the N-to-1 element synchronizes those streams by expected-timestamp-based logic. This means it lets all streams wait except for the one that provides the earliest next-expected timestamp. When that stream has passed one buffer, the next earliest-expected-timestamp is calculated, and we start back where we were, until all streams have reached EOS. There is a helper base class, called `GstCollectPads`, that will help you to do this.

Note, however, that this helper class will only help you with grabbing a buffer from each input and giving you the one with earliest timestamp. If you need anything more difficult, such as "don't-grab-a-new-buffer until a given timestamp" or something like that, you'll need to do this yourself.

Chapter 26. Writing a Manager

Managers are elements that add a function or unify the function of another (series of) element(s). Managers are generally a `GstBin` with one or more ghostpads. Inside them is/are the actual element(s) that matters. There is several cases where this is useful. For example:

- To add support for private events with custom event handling to another element.

- To add support for custom pad `_query ()` or `_convert ()` handling to another element.

- To add custom data handling before or after another element's data handler function (generally its `_chain ()` function).

- To embed an element, or a series of elements, into something that looks and works like a simple element to the outside world. This is particular handy for implementing sources and sink elements with multiple pads.

Making a manager is about as simple as it gets. You can derive from a `GstBin`, and in most cases, you can embed the required elements in the `_init ()` already, including setup of ghostpads. If you need any custom data handlers, you can connect signals or embed a second element which you control.

V. Appendices

This chapter contains things that don't belong anywhere else.

Chapter 27. Things to check when writing an element

This chapter contains a fairly random selection of things to take care of when writing an element. It's up to you how far you're going to stick to those guidelines. However, keep in mind that when you're writing an element and hope for it to be included in the mainstream GStreamer distribution, it *has to* meet those requirements. As far as possible, we will try to explain why those requirements are set.

27.1. About states

- Make sure the state of an element gets reset when going to `NULL`. Ideally, this should set all object properties to their original state. This function should also be called from _init.

- Make sure an element forgets *everything* about its contained stream when going from `PAUSED` to `READY`. In `READY`, all stream states are reset. An element that goes from `PAUSED` to `READY` and back to `PAUSED` should start reading the stream from the start again.

- People that use **gst-launch** for testing have the tendency to not care about cleaning up. This is *wrong*. An element should be tested using various applications, where testing not only means to "make sure it doesn't crash", but also to test for memory leaks using tools such as **valgrind**. Elements have to be reusable in a pipeline after having been reset.

27.2. Debugging

- Elements should *never* use their standard output for debugging (using functions such as `printf ()` or `g_print ()`). Instead, elements should use the logging functions provided by GStreamer, named `GST_DEBUG ()`, `GST_LOG ()`, `GST_INFO ()`, `GST_WARNING ()` and `GST_ERROR ()`. The various logging levels can be turned on and off at runtime and can thus be used for solving issues as they turn up. Instead of `GST_LOG ()` (as an example), you can also use `GST_LOG_OBJECT ()` to print the object that you're logging output for.

- Ideally, elements should use their own debugging category. Most elements use the following code to do that:

```
GST_DEBUG_CATEGORY_STATIC (myelement_debug);
#define GST_CAT_DEFAULT myelement_debug

[..]

static void
gst_myelement_class_init (GstMyelementClass *klass)
{
[..]
  GST_DEBUG_CATEGORY_INIT (myelement_debug, "myelement",
    0, "My own element");
}
```

At runtime, you can turn on debugging using the commandline option **--gst-debug=myelement:5**.

- Elements should use GST_DEBUG_FUNCPTR when setting pad functions or overriding element class methods, for example:

```
gst_pad_set_event_func (myelement->srcpad,
    GST_DEBUG_FUNCPTR (my_element_src_event));
```

This makes debug output much easier to read later on.

- Elements that are aimed for inclusion into one of the GStreamer modules should ensure consistent naming of the element name, structures and function names. For example, if the element type is GstYellowFooDec, functions should be prefixed with gst_yellow_foo_dec_ and the element should be registered as 'yellowfoodec'. Separate words should be separate in this scheme, so it should be GstFooDec and gst_foo_dec, and not GstFoodec and gst_foodec.

27.3. Querying, events and the like

- All elements to which it applies (sources, sinks, demuxers) should implement query functions on their pads, so that applications and neighbour elements can request the current position, the stream length (if known) and so on.

- Elements should make sure they forward events they do not handle with gst_pad_event_default (pad, parent, event) instead of just dropping them. Events should never be dropped unless specifically intended.

- Elements should make sure they forward queries they do not handle with gst_pad_query_default (pad, parent, query) instead of just dropping them.

27.4. Testing your element

- **gst-launch** is *not* a good tool to show that your element is finished. Applications such as Rhythmbox and Totem (for GNOME) or AmaroK (for KDE) *are*. **gst-launch** will not test various things such as proper clean-up on reset, event handling, querying and so on.

- Parsers and demuxers should make sure to check their input. Input cannot be trusted. Prevent possible buffer overflows and the like. Feel free to error out on unrecoverable stream errors. Test your demuxer using stream corruption elements such as `breakmydata` (included in gst-plugins). It will randomly insert, delete and modify bytes in a stream, and is therefore a good test for robustness. If your element crashes when adding this element, your element needs fixing. If it errors out properly, it's good enough. Ideally, it'd just continue to work and forward data as much as possible.

- Demuxers should not assume that seeking works. Be prepared to work with unseekable input streams (e.g. network sources) as well.

- Sources and sinks should be prepared to be assigned another clock then the one they expose themselves. Always use the provided clock for synchronization, else you'll get A/V sync issues.

Chapter 28. Porting 0.8 plug-ins to 0.10

This section of the appendix will discuss shortly what changes to plugins will be needed to quickly and conveniently port most applications from GStreamer-0.8 to GStreamer-0.10, with references to the relevant sections in this Plugin Writer's Guide where needed. With this list, it should be possible to port most plugins to GStreamer-0.10 in less than a day. Exceptions are elements that will require a base class in 0.10 (sources, sinks), in which case it may take a lot longer, depending on the coder's skills (however, when using the `GstBaseSink` and `GstBaseSrc` base-classes, it shouldn't be all too bad), and elements requiring the deprecated bytestream interface, which should take 1-2 days with random access. The scheduling parts of muxers will also need a rewrite, which will take about the same amount of time.

28.1. List of changes

- Discont events have been replaced by newsegment events. In 0.10, it is essential that you send a newsegment event downstream before you send your first buffer (in 0.8 the scheduler would invent discont events if you forgot them, in 0.10 this is no longer the case).

- In 0.10, buffers have caps attached to them. Elements should allocate new buffers with `gst_pad_alloc_buffer ()`. See Caps negotiation for more details.

- Most functions returning an object or an object property have been changed to return its own reference rather than a constant reference of the one owned by the object itself. The reason for this change is primarily thread-safety. This means effectively that return values of functions such as `gst_element_get_pad ()`, `gst_pad_get_name ()`, `gst_pad_get_parent ()`, `gst_object_get_parent ()`, and many more like these have to be free'ed or unreferenced after use. Check the API references of each function to know for sure whether return values should be free'ed or not.

- In 0.8, scheduling could happen in any way. Source elements could be `_get ()`-based or `_loop ()`-based, and any other element could be `_chain ()`-based or `_loop ()`-based, with no limitations. Scheduling in 0.10 is simpler for the scheduler, and the element is expected to do some more work. Pads get assigned a scheduling mode, based on which they can either operate in random access-mode, in pipeline driving mode or in push-mode. all this is documented in detail in Different scheduling modes. As a result of this, the bytestream object no longer exists. Elements requiring byte-level access should now use random access on their sinkpads.

- Negotiation is asynchronous. This means that downstream negotiation is done as data comes in and upstream negotiation is done whenever renegotiation is required. All details are described in Caps negotiation.

- For as far as possible, elements should try to use existing base classes in 0.10. Sink and source elements, for example, could derive from `GstBaseSrc` and `GstBaseSink`. Audio sinks or sources could even derive from audio-specific base classes. All existing base classes have been discussed in Pre-made base classes and the next few chapters.

- In 0.10, event handling and buffers are separated once again. This means that in order to receive events, one no longer has to set the `GST_FLAG_EVENT_AWARE` flag, but can simply set an event handling function on the element's sinkpad(s), using the function `gst_pad_set_event_function ()`. The `_chain ()`-function will only receive buffers.

- Although core will wrap most threading-related locking for you (e.g. it takes the stream lock before calling your data handling functions), you are still responsible for locking around certain functions, e.g. object properties. Be sure to lock properly here, since applications will change those properties in a different thread than the thread which does the actual data passing! You can use the `GST_OBJECT_LOCK ()` and `GST_OBJECT_UNLOCK ()` helpers in most cases, fortunately, which grabs the default property lock of the element.

- `GstValueFixedList` and all `*_fixed_list_* ()` functions were renamed to `GstValueArray` and `*_array_* ()`.

- The semantics of GST_STATE_PAUSED and GST_STATE_PLAYING have changed for elements that are not sink elements. Non-sink elements need to be able to accept and process data already in the GST_STATE_PAUSED state now (i.e. when prerolling the pipeline). More details can be found in Chapter 8.

- If your plugin's state change function hasn't been superseded by virtual start() and stop() methods of one of the new base classes, then your plugin's state change functions may need to be changed in order to safely handle concurrent access by multiple threads. Your typical state change function will now first handle upwards state changes, then chain up to the state change function of the parent class (usually GstElementClass in these cases), and only then handle downwards state changes. See the vorbis decoder plugin in gst-plugins-base for an example.

The reason for this is that in the case of downwards state changes you don't want to destroy allocated resources while your plugin's chain function (for example) is still accessing those resources in another thread. Whether your chain function might be running or not depends on the state of your plugin's pads, and the state of those pads is closely linked to the state of the element. Pad states are handled in the GstElement class's state change function, including proper locking, that's why it is essential to chain up before destroying allocated resources.

As already mentioned above, you should really rewrite your plugin to derive from one of the new base classes though, so you don't have to worry about these things, as the base class will handle it for you. There are no base classes for decoders and encoders yet, so the above paragraphs about state changes definitely apply if your plugin is a decoder or an encoder.

- `gst_pad_set_link_function ()`, which used to set a function that would be called when a format was negotiated between two `GstPad`s, now sets a function that is called when two elements are linked together in an application. For all practical purposes, you most likely want to use the function `gst_pad_set_setcaps_function ()`, nowadays, which sets a function that is called when the format streaming over a pad changes (so similar to `_set_link_function ()` in GStreamer-0.8).

If the element is derived from a `GstBase` class, then override the `set_caps ()`.

- `gst_pad_use_explicit_caps ()` has been replaced by `gst_pad_use_fixed_caps ()`. You can then set the fixed caps to use on a pad with `gst_pad_set_caps ()`.

Chapter 29. Porting 0.10 plug-ins to 1.0

You can find the list of changes in the Porting to 1.0
(http://cgit.freedesktop.org/gstreamer/gstreamer/tree/docs/random/porting-to-1.0.txt) document.

Chapter 30. GStreamer licensing

30.1. How to license the code you write for GStreamer

GStreamer is a plugin-based framework licensed under the LGPL. The reason for this choice in licensing is to ensure that everyone can use GStreamer to build applications using licenses of their choice.

To keep this policy viable, the GStreamer community has made a few licensing rules for code to be included in GStreamer's core or GStreamer's official modules, like our plugin packages. We require that all code going into our core package is LGPL. For the plugin code, we require the use of the LGPL for all plugins written from scratch or linking to external libraries. The only exception to this is when plugins contain older code under more liberal licenses (like the MPL or BSD). They can use those licenses instead and will still be considered for inclusion. We do not accept GPL code to be added to our plugins module, but we do accept LGPL-licensed plugins using an external GPL library. The reason for demanding plugins be licensed under the LGPL, even when using a GPL library, is that other developers might want to use the plugin code as a template for plugins linking to non-GPL libraries.

We also plan on splitting out the plugins using GPL libraries into a separate package eventually and implement a system which makes sure an application will not be able to access these plugins unless it uses some special code to do so. The point of this is not to block GPL-licensed plugins from being used and developed, but to make sure people are not unintentionally violating the GPL license of said plugins.

This advisory is part of a bigger advisory with a FAQ which you can find on the GStreamer website (http://gstreamer.freedesktop.org/documentation/licensing.html)

www.ingramcontent.com/pod-product-compliance
Lightning Source LLC
Chambersburg PA
CBHW060149060326
40690CB00018B/4040